FROM BLACKJACKS
TO BRIEFCASES

ROBERT MICHAEL SMITH

with a foreword by Scott Molloy

FROM BLACKJACKS TO BRIEFCASES

A History of
Commercialized Strikebreaking
and Unionbusting
in the United States

OHIO UNIVERSITY PRESS   ATHENS

Ohio University Press, Athens, Ohio 45701

12 11 10 09 08 07 06 05 04 03   5 4 3 2 1

Part of chapter 2 appeared in an earlier version as "King of the Strikebreakers: The Notorious Career of James A. Farley," *Labor's Heritage* 11 (spring/summer 2000): 20–37.

The discussion in chapter 2 of the McKees Rocks, Pennsylvania, Pressed Steel Car Company strike of 1909 appeared first in "King Pearl L. Bergoff Invades McKees Rocks," *Pennsylvania Heritage* 27 (summer 2002): 30–37.

Part of chapter 3 appeared in an earlier version as "Industrial Espionage Agencies: Ineffective or Deadly Anti-union Weapons?" *Mid-America* 80 (summer 1998).

Another part of chapter 3 appeared in an earlier version as "Spies against Labor: Industrial Espionage Agencies, 1855–1940," *Labor's Heritage* 5 (summer 1993).

An earlier version of chapter 4 appeared as "Using Knowledge Rather Than Goons: Labor Relations Consultants As Modern Union-Busters," *Michigan Academician* (fall 1996).

LIBRARY OF CONGRESS CATALOGING-IN-PUBLICATION DATA

Smith, Robert Michael, 1955-
    From blackjacks to briefcases : a history of commercialized strike-breaking and unionbusting in the United States / Robert Michael Smith with a foreword by Scott Molloy.
    p. cm.
    Includes bibliographical references and index.
    ISBN 0-8214-1465-8 (alk. paper)—ISBN 0-8214-1466-6 (pbk. : alk. paper)
    1. Strikebreakers—United States—History. 2. Union busting—United States—History. 3. Strikes and lockouts—United States—History I. Title.

HD5324 .S64 2003
331.89'4—dc21
                                                              2002030809

In memory of Sidney Jordan

CONTENTS

ILLUSTRATIONS

They have crossed the picket lines of history to a chorus of abuse: strikebreakers, blacklegs, knobsticks, and the contemporary euphemism, replacement workers. Then, of course, there is the inevitable, stinging, almost universal term *scab!*

Nearly every period of American history has produced detailed descriptions of them. The beloved American author Jack London once penned a short essay that became a thesaurus of uncomplimentary adjectives and metaphors for those who would cross a picket line to take the work of a striker. Every major walkout for 150 years seemed to incite participants to write and print their hatred for the despised trespassers.

Among those crossing over the line to commit labor's mortal sin, some were so desperate for work that the child's rhyme "sticks and stones may break my bones, but names will never hurt me" was appropriate. In some cases, gender, racial, and ethnic groups viewed strikes as opportunities to break into an industrial workforce. Still others, who came from foreign shores, could not distinguish the hateful words of strikers from others in the tower of Babel that was the English tongue. Then there were the professional scabs, who liked the adventure, thrill, and remuneration for combating those who would engage business, government, or ideology.

Professor Robert Smith navigates the thickets of this hostile subsection of labor-management relations without ignoring the puppets who strung their way through union gauntlets. He primarily trains his sights on the puppeteers who supplied these working-class Hessians. The detective agencies, secret services, and brokers in human misery that operated on local and national levels usually toiled in extreme secrecy. The author has undauntingly provided a generational sketch of these operators from the days of the infamous Pinkerton Agency to the legal boardrooms of today's unionbusters.

The consequences of these episodes are evident in the outcomes of many strikes, but the marching orders usually lack a return address. Rather than trying to retell every such incident, the author concentrates on the broad swath and implications of these industrial troubles. He mines the rich material in the records of government hearings that help dissolve the shadows around the strikebreaking business. He culls newspapers and documents across the landscape of American history to uncover the workings of Pinkerton agents and Pearl Bergoff, the king of strikebreakers himself, or the memos between a Fortune 500 company and its legal team authorizing proletarian replacements.

No other work that I am familiar with covers so much ground in such economical fashion, exposing the underpinnings of an underground world that few ever see or imagine. Every chapter contains blockbuster quotations from robber barons, captains of industry, their allies, and modern-day CEOs. We view the struggles of ordinary Americans for a better life from behind the scenes as management employs thugs, detectives, snitches, legal loopholes, and Freudian psychology. This work will become the convenient handbook for the distasteful but necessary look at the rearguard tactics that still too often shape American labor-management relations.

Scott Molloy
Associate Professor
Schmidt Labor Research Center
University of Rhode Island

INTRODUCTION

Beginning with the emergence of the United States as an industrial power in the years following the Civil War and continuing until today, much of the business community has adamantly resisted labor's efforts to bargain collectively. For the first half-century of this struggle industrialists held firmly to their "open shop" ideology and their belief that wages should be governed by the law of supply and demand. As workers challenged this intransigence beginning with the Great Railroad Strike of 1877, industrial violence reached a level that did not significantly abate until the sanctioning of collective bargaining by the federal government. Even after the passage of the Wagner Act in 1935, these forces continued to battle one another, although less violently.

In spite of the fact that they occasionally acquiesced to their workers' demands, over the years, anti-union employers maintained their dominant position. Their ability to cow their workers into submission resulted from the fact that they did not stand alone. Militia forces, the judicial system, and state, local, and federal authorities all lent their assistance. Social and economic factors such as the ups and downs of the business cycle, with its massive armies of unemployed, and the strong American belief in the sanctity of private property, also allowed these men to maintain their hegemony.

Along with these familiar defenders of the status quo, for more than a century employers relied upon professional strikebreaking agencies to solve their labor problems. Focusing on rank-and-file workers, union formation, specific strikes, and the culture of work, students of the labor story have unfortunately paid little attention to the business community's relationship with these agencies.[1] The underground nature of these firms and their secretive relationships with their clientele have made it nearly impossible for scholars to do more than mention the role these mercenaries played. Moreover, aside from labor-law experts, who have recently begun to focus on the legal implications of skirting national labor law, no one interested in labor relations has taken a broad look at unionbusting since the enactment of the Wagner Act. Even more important, no study has traced the evolution of this industry and its practitioners' machinations.[2]

In no other country has the struggle between management and its employees engendered a contingent of mercenaries who specialized in breaking strikes. Skillfully adapting their strategies to the changing social and economic climate as well as the evolving capital-labor relationship, anti-union entrepreneurs have been a part of the business community's arsenal from the bloody strikes of the last quarter of the nineteenth century to today. With lucrative business opportunities promised by employers' continuing reluctance to bargain collectively with their workforces, those who preyed upon industrial unrest demonstrated a remarkable ability to invent new services. With new tactics came new "Strikebreaker Kings," men who dominated this industry, at least for a while.

In the years after the Civil War, as a large and unruly industrial proletariat began to threaten the established order, private policing emerged as a professional, highly organized, and lucrative business. The first firm to offer policing services to frightened employers, the Pinkerton National Detective Agency, soon found itself competing with a growing number of similar agencies. To workers, however, the Pinkerton name became synonymous with unionbusting.

In an age when much of the public regarded workers' efforts to organize as un-American or even criminal, employers felt little need for subtlety. Moreover, before the establishment of professional public policing systems, not only did few question capital's right to protect its private property, most communities sanctioned informal police systems. For their part, employers recognized, as did the members of the United States Industrial Commission of 1902, that city police were dominated by a working-class constituency that made them "unwilling to enforce order effectively."[3]

Although the professional and efficient service they promised employers must have seemed a godsend, Pinkerton guards often proved more of a liability than an asset. Indeed, the violence associated with the introduction of such forces often generated hostility against their clients and public sympathy for the strikers. Following the Homestead Steel strike and the public condemnation and spate of "anti-Pinkerton" legislation that that debacle generated, some employers began to seek other means of labor control.

Around the turn of the century the muckraker F. B. McQuiston gave notice to a new departure in labor discipline when he pointed out to readers of the *Independent* that "within the past decade the strikebreaker has become indispensable to the successful mill operator."[4] What he was talking about was not the solitary black or immigrant worker who had been tricked into selling his class loyalty for the opportunity to work but armies of mercenaries whose function was to convince striking workers that their colleagues had returned to work. Employers were capable of looking after their own affairs, for strikebreaking was a time-honored occupation and most knew how to recruit such men. Still, many lacked the resolve and wherewithal to do so on their own. More so than the hired armed guards, these professionals often proved able allies.

Though some Americans regarded the armies of guards who surrounded strike-bound plants as remnants of a feudal past during which princes hired mercenaries to impose their will on others, much of the public looked upon strikebreakers differently. Many would have agreed with onetime president of Harvard University Charles W. Elliot, who referred to such men as "the heroes of American industry."[5] To Elliot and others, they represented the American worker who possessed the right to work wherever and for whomever he desired. Moreover, although the introduction of strikebreakers enraged striking workers and their allies, the public often proved indifferent to their arrival, for few dared challenge another major tenet of the American economic system: the businessman's right to hire whomever he desired. Glorified for their efforts, the captains of these mercenary armies, such as James A. Farley and Pearl L. Bergoff, earned not only national reputations but the title "King of the Strikebreakers." Representing a new departure in labor discipline, their names commonly appeared in newspapers and magazine articles, as did their opinions regarding industrial matters. Still, the disorder that went hand in hand with the arrival of such armies occasionally proved more important than those vaunted American economic axioms. Although strikebreaking troops and even armed guards continued to engage strikers in battle until the 1930s, as early as the first part of the new century these plug-uglies were already beginning to fall out of the favor of anti-union employers as the public became less and less tolerant of the violence that accompanied labor disputes.

Recognizing that a professional intelligence service that could supply information about the conditions, activities, and strategies of their enemies would be invaluable to employers, anti-union entrepreneurs increasingly began to deal in industrial espionage. Although spying on workers was a long-established practice, as the well-worn tenets of a laissez-faire economy gave way to concerns about workers, and muckrakers made businessmen wary of antagonizing the public, managers increasingly sought more subtle means to control their workforces. By the Depression decade, industrial espionage had become not only an accepted part of labor relations but the most important form of labor discipline services provided by anti-union specialists.

Reports completed by the Commission on Industrial Relations in 1915, a privately funded investigation into the steel strike of 1919, and those generated by the National Labor Relations Board and the La Follette Civil Liberties Committee make it clear that espionage agencies provided anti-union employers with an effective service. After two years of hearings, during which members of the La Follette committee called before Congress the officers and operatives of five of the nation's largest labor espionage agencies, their clients, and their victims, the committee concluded that espionage was "the most efficient method known to management to prevent unions from forming, to weaken them if they secure a foothold, and to wreck them when they try their strength."[6] Indeed, well ensconced within the ranks of workers and even within organized labor, spies, agents provocateurs, and missionaries succeeded in reducing countless unions to little more than debating societies during the Depression decade.

While the industrial upheaval of the late nineteenth and early twentieth centuries provided a wealth of business opportunities for anti-union agencies, the violence they spawned and the havoc they wreaked on the labor movement eventually exposed their tactics to the light of day. Not only were such agencies the subject of countless newspaper and muckraking articles, numerous state and federal inquiries also revealed to a shocked public the extent of this industry and the degree to which the business community had become dependent upon its services. Although the owners and officials of these agencies, as well as their clients, invoked the specter of communism when called on to explain their actions, it became clear that their tactics and functions were themselves un-American.

For much of this period, however, at least until the 1930s, the majority of the American public was not ready for such revelations. For most, the idea that the business community might be the aggressor was unfathomable. Consequently, until after World War II, these inquiries failed to generate any effective regulatory legislation. Although anti-union agencies remained free to practice their trade, after the La Follette Committee hearings employers voluntarily ended their dependence upon the suppliers of armed guards, strikebreakers, and even spies. While lawmakers failed to enact any regulatory legislation that might have hampered such agencies, the revelations generated by this Senate inquiry enraged the public, which, beginning with the economic collapse of 1929, no longer regarded the business community as unassailable.

After World War II, most workers were unaware that management had hired specialists to help them avoid unionization. As the capital-labor relationship became more institutionalized, labor-relations consulting agencies, attorneys, and industrial psychologists provided anti-union services to those employers who had not forgotten their opposition to organized labor. The newest "Strikebreaker Kings" included labor relations consultants such as Nate Shefferman, Alfred DeMaria, and Herbert Melnick. Rather than thugs, these modern unionbusters employed professionals to manipulate national labor laws as well as the minds of their clients' workers. Not only were their efforts far subtler, they could be disguised as constructive employee relations.

When Congress stumbled upon the business community's reliance upon these mercenaries in the mid-1950s, once again the anti-union industry's activities were dragged before the public. This time national lawmakers enacted regulatory legislation. Their efforts succeeded for at least a decade. Indeed, there is little evidence suggesting that employers relied upon anti-union services during the 1960s or the first part of the next decade.

Rather than acquiescing before congressional and public disapproval, anti-union professionals eventually adapted to this new environment. Moreover, by the late 1970s, the growing hostility toward unionism not only allowed these mercenaries to blatantly ignore regulatory legislation they found bothersome, but also led to the business community's rediscovery of their services. From the early 1980s to today, labor relations consultants have enabled their clients to claim victory in countless NLRB-sanctioned elections. Indeed, setbacks suffered by unions in workers' elections have been paralleled by the business community's growing reliance upon these mercenaries.

During the past decade, professional unionbusting has come full circle. Indeed, modern unionbusters have felt little pressure to refine their tactics as their predecessors had. In the anti-union environment of recent years, as the ability to subtly discourage clients' workers from unionizing no longer proved [as] important, many employers turned to more blatant forms of labor discipline services. Emboldened by a pro-business milieu which began as early as the Reagan years and still exists today, they began contracting not only with those agencies that specialized in supplying replacement workers but also with professional security firms whose operatives were little more than thugs. Indeed, the only difference between the Pinkerton Agency of the late nineteenth century or the Bergoff Service Bureau of the first part of the next century and today's anti-union professional is the latter's reliance upon modern technology.

FROM BLACKJACKS
TO BRIEFCASES

1

THE BUSINESS COMMUNITY'S MERCENARIES

The Era of Privately Paid Police

OUTRUNNING ESTABLISHED POLICE systems as they pushed into the frontier in the first part of the nineteenth century, Americans showed little hesitancy in relying upon informal mechanisms to maintain law and order. While elected sheriffs and the citizenry instilled industrial discipline and provided an effective ally before the industrial revolution, such systems often broke down when thousands of workers defied established rights of private property later in that century. Surely local authorities could not call upon citizens to march against their neighbors and friends to secure the businessman's right to operate his factory as he wished.

The public's inadequate mechanisms for disciplining large numbers of angry workers became clear during the Great Railroad Strike of 1877. Not only did local police fail to control strikers, most of the states affected by this dispute did not support an active militia or a state police force. Moreover, not until the Progressive era, when August Vollmer, head of the Berkeley, California, police department, launched a law enforcement reform campaign, did Americans confront the inadequacy of their policing systems.[1] To insure law and order, steps needed to be taken.

One response was the rise of the national guard. Less than two years after the bloody railroad strikes the National Guard Association was founded. The business community took an active interest in this organization, backing the establishment of armories throughout the country. In the fifteen years following the summer of 1877, national guard units took a role in quelling thirty-three labor disputes.[2] During these strike-laden years, besieged employers also began turning to private policing agencies for help. Such services fit easily into an age in which few questioned capital's right to take steps to protect its private property. With the rise of professional societies and the coming of the professional manager, this was also an era during which American businessmen began to show a preference for expertise and specialization. Moreover, when employers turned to private policing agencies, they were seeking a traditional solution to their problems. Undeterred by democratic restraints and financial concerns, such agencies operated completely at the business community's behest. Accountable only to their clients, they appeared to furnish an effective and efficient form of labor control. Surprisingly enough, in most cases private guards not only proved far from effective but often exacerbated an already volatile situation. Although their heyday came to an end at the dawn of the new century with the establishment of professional public police departments, they continued to provide mine owners in frontier environments with their unique form of social control well into the twentieth century.

Allan Pinkerton, the founder of the most famous detective agency in the United States, the Pinkerton National Detective Agency, was the first to foresee the profits to be earned by supplying professional armed guards to frightened businessmen. By the last decades of the nineteenth century Pinkerton guards were such a common sight at strikebound plants that "Pinkertons" became the eponym applied to all armed guards.

Pinkerton's early years provided no indication that he would become one of the best-known defenders of the propertied class. Born in Glasgow, Scotland, in the first part of the nineteenth century, he was raised in a filthy tenement district known as the Gorbals, the home of countless brothels and criminals of every sort. After his father, a police officer, died, he began working twelve-hour days as an apprentice in a pattern-making shop to support his family. Later, he apprenticed himself to a barrel maker and eventually joined the Cooper's Trade Union.[3]

Like many on the bottom of the industrial order, during the 1830s and 1840s he also involved himself in Chartism. Along with thousands he

Fig. 1.1 A young Allan Pinkerton opened a cooperage outside of Chicago after emigrating from England, but found himself drawn into detective work after stumbling upon a ring of counterfeiters and helping to bring them to justice. From Edward Levinson, *I Break Strikes! The Technique of Pearl L. Bergoff* (New York: Robert M. McBride and Company, 1935; rpt., New York: Arno and New York Times, 1969).

eventually fled England for the United States when the government, which regarded the Chartists' efforts to secure better lives for English workers as treasonous, made life difficult for these men. After the ship in which he crossed the Atlantic wrecked in a heavy storm, he found himself in Canada nearly destitute.

Urged to move to Chicago, Illinois, by a Scottish friend, he landed in that city in 1842. American freedoms seemed particularly appealing. "In my native country I was free in name, but a slave in fact," he wrote after his arrival.[4] Here he found work as a cooper for Lill's Brewery.

He dreamed of owning his own business, and in the following year he opened a cooperage in Dundee, Illinois. Employing eight apprentices, his business thrived, and he quickly established himself as a respected member of the community.[5] His placid life soon came unraveled as he became involved in police work.

Pinkerton's career as a detective began in 1847 when he accidentally stumbled onto a camp of counterfeiters hiding out in the woods near his shop. In the decades before the Civil War, laws regulating the national currency did not extend to the increasing number of state and independent bank notes. Compounding this chaotic situation, counterfeiters traveled the countryside selling fake money to those wanting to make a fast profit. Returning with the local sheriff, Pinkerton helped arrest the men.[6] When two local merchants, who were impressed by the heroic Scotsman and angered over the inadequacy of local police, asked him to watch for counterfeiters on a part-time basis, Pinkerton at first declined. But because of his vested interest in the economic survival of Dundee, or perhaps because policing traditions ran through his family, he later agreed.[7]

Although he continued to operate his cooperage, more and more he showed himself an able detective. For example, when a suspicious stranger arrived in Dundee, Pinkerton befriended him and then inquired about purchasing counterfeit money. When the newcomer handed over a stack of fake money, the young detective arrested him. "The country being new, and great sensations scarce, the affair was in everybody's mouth," Pinkerton wrote. He went on to note that he suddenly found himself "called upon, from every quarter, to undertake matters requiring the detective skill."[8]

Later, after he rescued two girls who had been kidnapped in Michigan and spirited to Illinois, the citizens of Cook County installed Pinkerton as deputy sheriff for Cook County.[9] Enthralled by his new skills and growing increasingly weary of barrel making, Pinkerton sold his cooperage, packed his household, and left for Chicago, where he accepted appointment as that city's first detective.[10]

The citizens of that city would not have his services for long, for he recognized that Chicago's lack of adequate policing provided lucrative opportunities for those skilled in police work. As in most large cities, Chicago's police department remained not only unprofessional but also dominated by politics and hindered by jurisdictional issues. In 1850, Pinkerton and a Chicago attorney, Edward Rucker, formed the Northwestern Police Agency.

Little is known about Rucker or the firm he cofounded. It seems likely that the rumor that he dropped out after a year was true.[11] What is certain is that eight years later Pinkerton established his own policing agency, Pinkerton's Protective Police Patrol. A small body of uniformed night watchmen, this force supplemented Chicago's police by providing night protection for hundreds of businesses. In their first year of operation they reported on more than 750 cases in which doors had been left unlatched or forcibly opened. Having been granted the power to arrest, they detained fifty-three individuals for crimes ranging from disorderly conduct to larceny that year. In addition to guarding mercantile establishments, warehouses, and factories, the Pinkerton Protective Patrol provided police protection for large outdoor events.[12]

For Allan Pinkerton, the move from providing watchmen for the protection of banks and merchants to supplying guards in times of labor disputes was an easy one. Like many Americans, he regarded union activity as not only criminal but contrary to American values. In his *Strikers, Communists, Tramps, and Detectives,* released in 1878, he wrote: "Every trade-union has for its vital principal, whatever is professed, the concentration of brute force to gain certain ends."[13]

The next two decades witnessed an unprecedented level of industrial violence as workers disrupted the smooth operation of business on more than twenty-two thousand occasions.[14] In the midst of America's industrial expansion his business thrived as strike work came to occupy the majority of the Protective Patrol's time.[15] He had indeed come full circle since his Chartist days.

A miner's strike at Braidwood, Illinois, in September of 1866, provided Pinkerton guards with their first experience battling angry workers.[16] Eight years later, they returned to this small mining community when the Chicago, Wilmington, and Vermilion Company requested their services after their miners walked out in protest over wage cuts. Accompanied by Allan Pinkerton, the first contingent of twenty guards arrived in late June. After a boardinghouse caught fire the day the walkout began, local operators hired thirty more. Each carried a rifle or musket supplied by the Pinkerton Agency and received a good wage for the time: four dollars a day plus room and board.[17]

Although the Pinkerton men were well armed, the citizens of this community soon rendered them powerless. For example, when the coal operators requested that officials grant their mercenaries police privileges, the mayor and sheriff not only turned down their appeal but deputized local striking miners, who promised to protect private property. Later, after the mayor refused to allow the Pinkerton men to parade in the streets, the sheriff confiscated their weaponry, noting that he did not propose "to have a lot of strangers dragooning a quiet town with deadly weapons in their hands." He claimed that he feared the miners "a good deal less than the Chicago watchmen."[18] Demonstrating little sympathy for the Pinkerton forces, he arrested and fined a number of them, including one for hitting an elderly lady. The fine amounted to one hundred dollars.[19]

For their part, strikers and their sympathizers showed little but contempt for this army. On one occasion, a group of women attacked Allan Pinkerton. He drove off, what one Chicago newspaper labeled, an "amazon mob" by "using the butt of his revolver and discharging one chamber."[20] In short, working people, their families, and their elected officials refused to submit to a mercenary army brought in by absentee mine owners. Their experience in Braidwood led the agency to shun industrial work for the next few years.[21]

The Pinkerton Agency's hiatus from labor work did not last long. With Allan Pinkerton's death in 1884, the agency reentered the field of guarding industrial facilities during strikes.[22]

Although the Protective Patrol brought in a steady income over the years, to Allan Pinkerton and his eldest son, William, it remained secondary to the detection of crime. Robert Pinkerton, however, urged that they expand this service, convinced that future fortunes lay in that direction. He proved an astute businessman, for the economic downturn of the 1880s ushered in one of the most violent eras in American labor history. Throughout that decade and into the next, sparked by declining wages, layoffs, and higher prices, workers protested what they considered ruthless exploitation. Frightened by this militancy, employers like the coal mine operators in the Hocking Valley of southeastern Ohio turned to the Pinkerton Agency for help.[23] The arrival of a unit of Pinkerton guards only antagonized the miners and the citizens of that part of Ohio, who petitioned Governor George Hoadly in 1884 to remove them.[24] Once again the Pinkertons found their authority compromised by a community that resented their entrance into local affairs. A number of arrests eventually followed their introduction. At New Straitsville, for instance, authorities charged twenty-five Pinkertons with carrying concealed weapons and "unlawfully usurping the office of constable." They eventually dropped this case, allowing the guards to keep their weapons, provided that they only use them for self-defense.[25] Not until this dispute ended during the second week of February of the next year did the Pinkerton men leave.[26]

Even as their reputation grew and their clientele expanded, the Pinkerton guards' ability as an effective unionbusting force was blown well out of proportion. For example, when molders and foundry men walked out of the McCormick Harvester Company plants in the early spring of 1885, the Pinkertons' presence only enraged the strikers. As fights broke out almost daily outside the factory's main gates, the Pinkertons often got the worst of it. Strikers and their sympathizers not only attacked scabs as they rode in McCormick omnibuses to the besieged plant; on one occasion they even stopped a busload of Pinkerton men and severely beat them. They then made off with a case of Winchester rifles. More than once, company officials called upon local police officials to protect the guards.[27] Forced to restore a 15 percent wage cut, Cyrus H. McCormick vowed to break the union.

With the new year, McCormick replaced his employees with non-union labor, prompting a strike which only intensified when three hundred Pinkertons were brought in to protect the new workforce. Every day that spring, pickets clashed with these guards along the so-called Black Road, a street leading to the plant. The guards' inability to control the strikers led to at least one man's death. On April 9, as a mob pressed in on them, the Pinkertons fired into the threatening crowd. One of the bullets struck George Roth, an old man who stood fifty feet away.

Fig. 1.2 Pinkerton guards standing watch at a mine near Buchtel, Ohio, during the Hocking Valley Coal Strike of 1884. Collection of the Ohio Historical Society.

After he died later that afternoon, authorities arrested four Pinkerton agents.[28] The strike ended three days later when company officials conceded to the strikers.

In the fall of 1886 Pinkerton guards further enraged these same citizens when they tangled with that city's packinghouse workers and their union, the Knights of Labor. In early October, 152 Pinkerton men guarded the packing plants and a large group of strikebreakers brought into town by the Packers' Association.[29] Their ranks swelled to five hundred before this dispute ended.[30] The Packers' Association quartered these men in one of the packinghouses, which soon took on the appearance of a military camp. Armed with Winchesters, sentinels patrolled the perimeter,

Fig. 1.3 Pinkerton guards proved little deterrent to the violence that erupted outside the gates of the McCormick Harvester Works during a strike there in 1886. Courtesy of the Illinois Labor History Society.

barring entrance to anyone without a pass. Inside this compound, army veterans drilled recruits in military tactics. In the building one could find a barracks with rows of cots and a mess room. "The whole scene," wrote one reporter, "is a very martial one, and all the men are under strict discipline of soldiers in camp."[31]

Rather than professional soldiers the Pinkerton men acted more like a marauding army. Often drunk, they insulted citizens and threatened them with their Winchesters, eventually provoking the community's ire. Convinced that many of these men were "thieves, tramps and disreputable characters," police officials arrested a number of them.[32] For their part, strikers regarded them with justified contempt. In early October, for instance, a gathering crowd refused to disperse when ordered to do so, and taunted the large force of Pinkertons dispatched to quell this demonstration. With bloodshed imminent, a local police official ordered the Pinkertons back and single-handedly broke up the throng.[33] After countless similar incidents an editor for the *Chicago Tribune* spoke for many when he explained to his readers that the end of this strike meant that the Pinkertons "can now draw their pay and go home."[34]

Their last days in the city, however, witnessed one of the most violent episodes of this strike. On October 19, Pinkerton guards exploded when sullen strikers, disgruntled over their union's unexpected capitulation, threw stones and hurled epithets at the guards' train as it prepared to depart. The frightened Pinkertons leveled their rifles at the gathering crowd and then, after their commander fired a warning shot, opened fire.[35] Amazingly only one man, Terence Begley, was killed. The enraged strikers quickly surrounded the Pinkerton men and stripped and beat a number of them.[36] Later, after William Pinkerton ordered them to surrender, several guards turned themselves in to police authorities. Owing to the efforts of the agency, however, no one was punished for this crime.[37] In early November, the state militia arrived to keep order. The soldiers easily controlled the crowds that bristled before the Pinkertons. Indeed, the strikers seemed pleased that the militia units "were to take the place of the hated Pinkerton guards," according to the *New York Times*.[38]

Although two innocent men lost their lives at the hands of Pinkerton guards in little more than a year, lawmakers in Illinois remained reluctant to respond. Shortly after the latter incident, backed by a critical press, the Illinois state legislature rejected a bill outlawing the introduction of private police into industrial disputes.[39] The sanctity of private property proved so important that when Democratic nominee for governor, John M. Palmer, asked why had "the state . . . become such an object of such contempt that standing armies are raised in its midst," few paid attention.[40] The year after the stockyard strike, the Knights of Labor drafted a platform demanding that detectives be banned from strike areas. Terence Powderly, head of this union, insisted that militia units be brought into these areas instead. In the *New York Times*, officials of the Pinkerton Agency responded by arguing that strikes were not a concern of the state but a private matter between those who wished to destroy property and those who wanted to protect it.[41] Most seemed to agree, as little came of the Knights' efforts. With few curbs on the activities of the Pinkerton men, violence continued unabated.

Less than three months after Terence Begley lost his life, Pinkerton guards inadvertently killed another bystander during the Jersey City coal wharves strike.[42] In early January of 1887, when coal handlers abandoned their posts after the Philadelphia and Reading Railroad announced a wage cut of two and a half cents an hour, railroad officials responded by bringing in hundreds of strikebreakers. They also turned to the Pinkerton Agency, which, according to a *New York Times* reporter, supplied an army of more than one hundred and fifty "big, strapping, courageous men," who looked "very formidable, with their cartridge belts and heavy revolvers strapped around their waists."[43] The secretary of the Jersey City Police Board admitted that he issued badges to 101 members of the Pinkerton Detective Agency on January 17.[44] That same day, the courts swore in more than two hundred Pinkerton men as federal marshals in Bayonne. Carrying Winchesters, revolvers, and nightsticks, they turned the railroad property and surrounding area into an armed camp.[45]

In both cities, violence followed the introduction of these men. Citing his city's charter, which stipulated that special police must be residents of the city for two years before appointment, the mayor of Jersey City, Orestes Cleveland, demanded their removal.[46] The next day his fears were realized when guards in the employ of this agency shot and killed a fourteen-year-old boy, Thomas Hogan, an innocent bystander.[47] That evening police officials arrested Patrick Sheehey, Daniel Cabill, Mortimer Morriarity, and Samuel D. Neff, all members of this mercenary army. Rumors circulated, however, that two other Pinkerton men left town on a westbound train.[48] In Bayonne, after police officials arrested a guard for beating a citizen senseless, only cool-headed police officials prevented an angry crowd from lynching him.[49] Although coal began to move across the Hudson River after the introduction of Pinkerton forces, the Hogan murder solidified labor sentiment around the region. A sympathetic waterfront strike dramatically slowed this supply as the International Boatmen's Union and coal handlers on the other side of the bay refused to handle nonunion coal.[50] In Bayonne, members of the city council denounced the "monopolistic coal kings" for "sending an armed body of Pinkerton forces to protect 'scab' labor." Community members responded by maintaining a boycott against the Pinkertons and contributing heavily to the strike fund.[51] As editors of one national magazine argued that reliance upon such mercenary forces was evidence that the "nation had sunk into a form of medieval barbarism similar to the feudalism of the twelfth century," anger also spread outside the strike area.[52] Early the next month, Jersey City officials indicted three of the four Pinkerton guards. Now, not only did their colleagues no longer venture beyond the railroad compound, company officials moved the guards to the rear of the Delaware, Lackawana, and Western yard.[53] At their trial in early June, the prosecution requested a verdict against only one of the defendants. Because of a lack of evidence, the jury found him innocent.[54]

The conduct of the Pinkerton men during this dispute as well as others of the last two decades of the nineteenth century led to a growing antipathy against the agency. Editors for the official organ of the Knights of Labor spoke for wage earners in 1886 when they argued that these guards were "from the lowest class of society—a class notoriously unprincipled, worthless and venal."[55] While the Farmers' Alliance movement in Indiana, South Dakota, and Washington denounced "Pinkertonism," the Union Labor party went one step further, insisting upon the "complete obliteration of that public infamy known as the Pinkerton Detective Agency."[56] The public and their representatives also began to take notice. Disgusted by the actions of Pinkerton guards during the New York Central Railroad strike of 1890, one of New York's representatives, John Quinn, presented a petition to fellow congressmen asking that they outlaw the private guard industry. Little came of his efforts, however.[57] The federal government finally considered legislative action when Thomas Watson, the Populist representative from Georgia, introduced a proposal in early 1892 to the House to outlaw hired guards. Only after William Jennings Bryan eloquently proclaimed, "Governments are organized to protect life and property. These functions should not be transferred to private individuals and hired detectives until we are ready to acknowledge government a failure," did the national legislature enact this resolution.[58] Still, a thorough investigation into the armed guard industry awaited one of the bloodiest labor disputes of the late nineteenth century.

When workers walked out of the Carnegie steel works at Homestead, Pennsylvania, in early July of 1892, plant manager Henry Clay Frick erected a barbed-wire fence around the factory and contracted for three hundred Pinkerton men to act as guards. Like many managers, he had little faith in public policing mechanisms. He remembered that during a small strike three years earlier, local police "were driven off, their hats and coats taken from them, and they were driven back to Pittsburgh."[59] The Pinkerton brothers recruited their army from New York, Chicago, and Philadelphia. From Youngstown, Ohio, where they gathered, they floated their guards down the Monongahela River on three barges. Under the command of F. L. Hines, a ten-year Pinkerton employee, this detachment included a number of Civil War veterans, who, according to one guard, "did not attempt to exercise authority but carried themselves very professionally."[60] Although the agency sent along a large cache of weapons and ammunition, they did not encourage violence. Recalling his trip down the river, this same man said, "We were told we should fire no arms and if we got a few bricks on the head . . . we should not say much about it."[61] Once again the importation of Pinkerton forces into a strike zone would not go uncontested.

As they landed at Homestead in the early morning hours of July 6, hundreds of angry strikers greeted them at the water's edge, and shooting soon broke out. After a twelve-hour siege, in which the strikers set the river ablaze with oil and fired a Civil War cannon acquired from the town green at the invaders, Frick's mercenaries finally surrendered. Marching them through town, an enraged citizenry vented their wrath against these men. "The character of the injuries inflicted upon the Pinkertons . . . were too indecent and brutal to describe," a House committee later reported.[62] In this most famous of labor struggles, three Pinkerton guards and ten strikers perished. This battle on the banks of the Monongahela River sparked an outcry best expressed in William W. Delaney's popular ballad "Father Was Killed by the Pinkerton Men":

'Twas in a Pennsylvania town not very long ago
Men struck against reductions in their pay
Their millionaire employer with philanthropic show
Had closed the mills till starved they would obey
They fought for home and right to live where they had toiled so long
But ere the sun had set some were laid low
There are hearts now sadly grieving by that sad and bitter wrong
God help them for it was a cruel blow
God help them tonight in their hour of affliction
Pray for him who they'll never see again
Hear the poor orphans tell their sad story[63]

With public interest and debate over this incident at a fever pitch, the Populists, who were meeting in St. Louis for their nominating convention, incorporated an anti-Pinkerton plank into their platform.[64] Clearly

Fig. 1.4 Angry strikers repulse three hundred Pinkerton guards as they attempt to land at the Homestead steel plant in July 1892. Originally appeared in *Frank Leslie's Illustrated Weekly,* July 14, 1892. Reproduced from *"The River Ran Red": Homestead 1892,* David P. Demarest Jr., general editor (Pittsburgh: University of Pittsburgh Press, 1992).

FULL SURRENDER.

--- --- ---

The Pinkerton Detectives
Marched From the Barges
Defeated.

--- --- ---

WORKMEN ALLOWED THEM LIFE.

--- --- ---

But Heaped all Sorts of Indignities on
the Prisoners.

--- --- ---

COMPELLED TO RUN A GAUNTLET.

--- --- ---

They Were Kept Prisoners in the Rink Until
Late Last Night.

--- --- ---

THEN STARTED TO PITTSBURGH.

--- --- ---

Full Story of the Determined Attack on the Boats.

--- --- ---

WAS NO RESISTANCE IN THE AFTERNOON.

Fig. 1.5 Although they spared the lives of the subdued Pinkerton guards, enraged strikers and their sympathizers vented their wrath against those they regarded as hired gunmen. Originally appeared in the *Pittsburgh Post*, July 7, 1892. Reproduced from *"The River Ran Red": Homestead 1892*, David P. Demarest Jr., general editor (Pittsburgh: University of Pittsburgh Press, 1992).

obvious that the two major parties would now have to grapple with the issue of Pinkertonism, both houses of Congress established subcommittees to investigate the battle on the Monongahela River.

On the day following the Homestead battle, members of the House adopted a resolution to investigate the activities of Pinkerton men "in the present instance, and the causes and conditions of the sanguinary conflict now going on at Homestead, Pa."[65] Committee members began their investigation by traveling to the scene of the incident, where they interviewed striking workers, townspeople, Pinkerton guards, local law enforcement officials, Henry Clay Frick, and Robert and William Pinkerton.[66] Robert, who agreed to answer fifty questions presented to the committee by the executive board of the Knights of Labor, dismissed a number of rumors, including the story that his men sheeted the barges with iron plating in anticipation of trouble.[67] The Pinkerton brothers also submitted a lengthy written statement blaming the Homestead debacle on the striking steel workers and reminded members of the inquiry that their actions were "legally justifiable under the laws of the United States and the state of Pennsylvania."[68] The Grand Master Workman of the Knights of Labor, Terence Powderly, also appeared before the committee. Convinced that Pinkerton guards killed his wife during an earlier disturbance, he angrily charged: "When the Pinkertons fire upon the people they do so from behind the breast-works of capital."[69] Committee members negated much of his testimony, noting that his "charges were based almost entirely on hearsay evidence."[70] The committee found further reason to dismiss much of what he said when he failed to reappear after he promised to return with documentation.[71]

The Senate waited until late fall to begin its inquiry.[72] Hearings were held in Chicago, Pittsburgh, and New York, the senators swearing in their first witness on November 17, 1892. In addition to Frank Murray, superintendent of the Pinkertons' Chicago office, Patrick Foley, the head of the Pinkerton Protective Patrol, also appeared and claimed that he hired only responsible men and that they did not tolerate drunkenness. In addition to industrial leaders who engaged the Pinkerton Agency, committee members called on a handful of workers, who provided the most dramatic testimony. "The English language is inadequate to express the hatred of the men in regards to them," one proclaimed.[73] Other witnesses included Frank Hitchcock, a United States marshall who argued

Fig. 1.6 Shortly after the battle ended, the Homestead Strike became a national issue. As editorialists and politicians voiced their opinions, national magazines provided complete coverage of the dispute. Originally appeared in *Frank Leslie's Illustrated Weekly,* July 14, 1892. Reproduced from *"The River Ran Red": Homestead 1892,* David P. Demarest Jr., general editor (Pittsburgh: University of Pittsburgh Press, 1992).

that the utilization of Pinkerton guards often became "an aggravation instead of a mediator," and Robert W. McClaughry, general superintendent of the Chicago Police Department, who claimed that employers in his city turned to detective agencies because the city found it "impossible to provide a police force large enough to meet all the wants of business."[74] During hearings in New York, Robert Pinkerton defended the Pinkerton name, saying that only three people had been killed during the twenty years in which they were involved in strike work. Although he believed that workers possessed the right to strike, he made it clear that his job was to protect property and those workers who opted not to strike.[75]

In spite of the anti-Pinkerton rhetoric that dominated the proceedings, the overriding concern for private property influenced much of Congress's thinking. Members of the House committee made this clear when they argued that the officers of the Carnegie Company stood upon firm legal ground in employing Pinkerton guards, as long as they did not "trespass upon the rights of persons or property of others."[76] They also pointed out that the hiring of armed guards was legal and that the striking steelworkers, in resisting the landing of the Pinkerton army, "violated the laws of Pennsylvania, for which they are answerable to the courts of the state."[77] Backed by the conviction that organized labor remained un-American, they responded the only way they could have. Congress did, however, draft a bill prohibiting the federal government and officers of the District of Columbia from employing Pinkerton guards under any circumstances.[78] They also made it clear that the states could regulate the employment of Pinkerton watchmen within their jurisdictions.[79] Still, after two inquiries, national legislators remained reluctant to step between employers and their mercenaries. Far from a failure, however, the congressional investigations of 1892 went a long way toward not only awakening the American people to the tactics of privately paid armed guards, but also prompting state lawmakers to legislate against their activities.

Even before the Homestead incident, several states enacted legislation to regulate armed guards within their borders. As early as 1885, for example, a state assemblyman in Pennsylvania introduced legislation to end the "Pinkerton system" in his state. Although his efforts proved a failure, the growth of the armed guard industry and their increasing role in the labor violence of those years prompted other lawmakers to take action.[80] By the end of the decade, Montana and Wyoming established constitutional provisions forbidding the importation of nonresidents for police work. The state of Missouri passed similar legislation in 1889, and Georgia followed the next year.[81] The battle along the Monongahela only added a new urgency to legislators' efforts.

In the months after the Homestead incident lawmakers across the nation enacted a host of bills that came to be known as "anti-Pinkerton" laws.[82] In Illinois, Governor John P. Altgeld devoted a part of his biennial speech of 1893 to the evils of Pinkertonism. Since the presence of such a force "tends to provoke riot and disorder," state officials should, he argued, "prohibit the use of these armed mercenaries by private corporations or individuals."[83] That same year, the state legislature made it illegal for police officials or corporate authorities to appoint anyone to act as a special constable, deputy sheriff, or special policeman who had not been a resident of the county in which they were to be employed for one year before the appointment.[84] The growing pressure exerted by the public can best be seen in Pennsylvania. Legislators in this state passed an armed guard bill without a dissenting vote in 1893.[85] By the last year of the nineteenth century, twenty-six states prohibited the importation of armed men from neighboring territories.[86] Whereas the laws enacted prior to 1892 prohibited the use of nonresidents as police officers, many of those enacted after this date referred specifically to detective agencies and in some instances even to the Pinkerton National Detective Agency.[87]

Although Robert Pinkerton was initially undaunted by these legislatorial efforts, within a year after the battle along the Monongahela River, a spokesman for the agency declared that the "work of supplying watchmen [during labor disputes] is extremely dangerous and undesirable and for that reason we prefer not to furnish watchmen in such cases."[88] In fact, as early as the middle of August 1892, Pinkerton guards were conspicuously absent during a New York Central Railroad strike. Two years earlier, Pinkerton men fired into a picket line during a walkout on that same line.[89] For the image-conscious Pinkerton National Detective Agency, the realization that many Americans questioned the presence of private armies for hire in a modern republic provided the impetus it needed to end its armed guard service. Involved in other pursuits, including the apprehension of criminals, the nation's leading detective agency could not risk further condemnation.

Those employers who remained hostile to unions did not stand alone, however. In an environment in which public police services proved inadequate, private policing agencies flourished. In 1871, John Boland and John Mooney established the firm of Mooney and Boland. This agency operated mostly along the West Coast.[90] Shortly after Pinkerton guards battled striking coal miners in Braidwood, Illinois, George H. Thiel set up the Thiel Agency in St. Louis. Business proved so good he later opened offices in New York, Chicago, Kansas City, St. Paul, and Portland, Oregon.[91] Among his many clients were the Illinois Central Railroad and the silver-mine owners in the Coeur d'Alene region of Idaho. During a work stoppage there in the summer of 1892 his men could be found working hand in hand with the Pinkerton Agency to bring that strike to an end.[92]

By 1893, Chicago alone could boast of more than twenty such agencies, including the U.S. Detective Agency.[93] Organized more than a decade earlier by Matt and Ross Pinkerton, its clients included the Morton Frog and Crossing Company, Carnegie Steel, the Wabash Railroad, and the Baltimore and Ohio Railroad. In 1885, its well-armed men played a major role in a lumber strike in Bay City, Michigan.[94] In 1892, it sent over twenty guards to Cleveland, Ohio, to provide protection during the streetcar strike of that year.[95] Other firms included the Illinois Detective Agency, the Standard Detective Agency, Alexander's Detective Agency, the American Detective Service, and the Veteran's Police Patrol and Detective Agency, which employed only veterans and their sons. The principal of this latter firm, John L. Manning, furnished more than one hundred guards to the Western Indiana Railroad Company and thirty more to the Wabash Railroad Company when their switchmen walked off the job in 1886.[96]

After the Homestead debacle, although some private policing agencies found ways to circumvent regulatory legislation and continued to offer their services to frightened employers, much of the business community came to rely less and less on private police. In isolated mining communities, however, private mercenaries remained a viable alternative well into the twentieth century. Such environments lacked adequate policing mechanisms, and major employers demanded near-complete control over the small towns and their residents. One of the most notorious armed-guard agencies, the Baldwin-Felts Agency, provided labor discipline services to mine owners in the hills of West Virginia and, on at least two occasions, to mine operations in Colorado. Founded by William G. Baldwin and Thomas L. Felts and based in southern West Virginia, in the small town of Bluefield, the agency began supplying guards to railroads and coal-mine operators as early as 1890.[97] In this frontier environment mountaineers frequently robbed freight trains as they made their way through the narrows and hollers of the southern part of the state. This practice ended, according to one student of West Virginia's history, "after the Baldwin-Felts men had killed a few such thieves and sent a number to prison." Within a few years the Baldwin-Felts Agency extended its services to West Virginia's expanding coal industry.[98] Although mine operators in this region had long relied upon their own men to act as deputy sheriffs, they soon discovered that this agency provided a more effective service. With offices situated on major railroad trunks, it could dispatch its armed men throughout the coal fields quickly.[99] For the Baldwin-Felts Agency it proved only a short step from guarding trains and coal tipples to providing the coal barons of this region with an effective labor discipline service.

One of the largest mine operators in this part of the state, Justus Collins, first turned to this agency for guards to protect his property in 1893. Less than ten years later, he utilized these same men to break a UMWA-sponsored strike. After joining his fellow operators, who agreed to enforce a thirty-day lockout, in June of 1902 he broke ranks by bringing in one hundred and fifty scab workers. Protected by forty Baldwin-Felts men, who guarded the iron gates to the mine and manned searchlights and a machine gun mounted upon the coal tipple, he reaped a fortune as his strikebreakers mined coal throughout that summer. This strike proved a boon not only to Collins, but also to the Baldwin-Felts Agency. In the wake of this success, more and more mine owners turned to this agency to end their labor difficulties.[100]

Found in nearly every mining community in the southern part of West Virginia by 1910, Baldwin-Felts guards provided the mine owners with a feudal-like control over their workers.[101] Under the orders of the mine operators these men policed the remote mining camps, guarded the payroll, collected rents, and often determined access to company towns,

Fig. 1.7 Thomas L. Felts, the most feared man in the coal-producing sections of West Virginia, was a founder of and later the driving force behind the Baldwin-Felts Detective Agency. From Howard B. Lee, *Bloodletting in Appalachia: The Story of West Virginia's Four Major Mine Wars and Other Thrilling Incidents of Its Coal Fields* (Morgantown: West Virginia University Press, 1969).

barring gamblers, prostitutes, and union organizers.[102] Once able to move freely around the state—after 1907—Baldwin-Felts thugs harassed union organizers from the time they stepped off the train until they left.[103] Two years later the UMWA acknowledged defeat by discouraging organizers from even entering southern West Virginia.[104] By 1912, Thomas Felts claimed that his men had eliminated "all semblance of unionism" in that part of the state. Felts's boast rang true, for the following year a satisfied client credited this agency with ridding much of West Virginia of union men and sympathizers.[105] As late as 1923, the United States Coal Commission concluded that "without the consent of the operators, a union organizer can do little more than ride on a train and look out the windows."[106]

Like those strikes in which the Pinkerton Agency participated, the introduction of guards in the employ of the Baldwin-Felts Agency eventually provoked strikers. For example, shortly after Felts boasted of his guards' prowess, the miners in Kanawha County rose up in what came to be known as the Paint Creek–Cabin Creek strike of 1912–13, in protest against his guards' brutality as well as his client's refusal to increase the miners' pay.[107] In early May of that first year, tensions reached their boiling point when Tom Felts increased his force along the two creeks to three hundred men to protect strikebreakers arriving from New York.[108] Bringing with them trained bloodhounds, the first reinforcements arrived on May 10, 1912.[109] Led by Albert and Lee Felts, younger brothers of the head of the agency, many of these men could boast of lengthy criminal records, and a few had at least one "notch" on their guns.[110] During the early phase of this dispute, in addition to escorting strikebreakers, Baldwin-Felts men constructed concrete forts throughout the valleys and equipped them with machine guns. On Cabin Creek, they placed one such weapon on a building owned by the Carbon Fuel Company. From portholes this gun could sweep the valley in all directions.[111]

Fig. 1.8   Heavily armed Baldwin-Felts guards on patrol in the Paint Creek District during the West Virginia Coal Wars of 1912–13. From Kyle McCormick, *The New-Kanawha River and the Mine War of West Virginia* (Charleston: Mathews Printing and Lithographing Company, 1959).

Fig. 1.9 Baldwin-Felts men in the Cabin Creek Strike District during the Paint Creek–Cabin Creek Strike. Armed with a machine gun, they commanded this hollow from a well-fortified gun emplacement. From Howard B. Lee, *Bloodletting in Appalachia: The Story of West Virginia's Four Major Mine Wars and Other Thrilling Incidents of Its Coal Fields* (Morgantown: West Virginia University Press, 1969).

Rather than providing order, the Baldwin-Felts Agency contributed to the violence that marred this strike. According to one newspaper reporter, "No class of men on earth [was more] cordially hated by the miners than these same guards who are engaged to protect them from outsiders."[112] Covering the strike for a Socialist newspaper, Ralph Chaplin captured the miners' antipathy in his poem entitled "Mine Guard":

You Cur? How can you stand so calm and still
And careless while your brothers strive and bleed?
What hellish, cruel, crime-polluted creed
Has taught you thus to do your master's will,
Whose guilty gold has damned your soul until
You lick his boots and fawn to do his deed—
To pander to his lust of boundless greed,
And guard him while his cohorts crush and kill?
Your brutish crimes are like a rotten flood—
The beating, raping, murdering you've done—
You psychopathic coward with a gun:
The worms would scorn your carcass in the mud;
A bitch would blush to hail you as a son—
You loathsome outcast, red with fresh-spilled blood.[113]

Although the Baldwin-Felts Agency earned nearly five hundred dollars a day as they battled striking miners along these two creeks, this bloody war threatened the agency's reputation and the legal system upon which its business rested.[114] Strikers killed several of its guards during a number of engagments, including the Battle of Mucklow, in the summer of 1912. In this skirmish in which twelve strikers and four guards lost their lives, the combatants exchanged thousands of shots. The *Charleston Daily Mail* headlined its account of this incident "A Regular Hurricane of Bullets Awakened the Echoes at Mucklow." Editors for this paper spoke for many of the strikers when they reported that a miner would just as soon "pick off a mine guard or mine official as he would eat his dinner."[115] Moreover, the public came to learn about the brutality of the mine owners' mercenaries through inquiries sponsored by the state of West Virginia and the United States Senate.[116] During this latter inquiry, for example, senators heard that one night in early February 1913 the local sheriff, a coal operator, and fourteen guards machine-gunned a strikers' tent colony at Holly Grove from an armored train known as the "Bull Moose Special."[117] Mine guard Lee Calvin told congressional investigators that after the train passed through the village, one mine owner remarked: "We gave them hell and had a lot of fun. Let's back up and give them another round."[118]

On other occasions, according to the chairman of this investigation, Democratic senator James E. Martine, "these trains would run up to a village, usually a single street along the railroad track, the mine guards would fire a couple of rifle shots from the cars to incite the strikers to return fire, and then the machine guns would be brought into action."[119] In return for the Holly Grove incident, the miners ambushed a company of Baldwin-Felts thugs at the Mucklow mining camp on February 10, 1913. In this second attack on this mining community at least two men lost their lives.[120] Before the year was over, state lawmakers enacted the Wertz Bill, making it unlawful for any "deputy or deputies to act as, or perform any duties in the capacity of guards . . . for any private individual or, firm or corporation."[121] The men of the Baldwin-Felts Agency continued to rule southwestern West Virginia, however, for few took the Wertz Bill seriously, as legislators failed to include a penalty clause.[122]

Even if they had been able to enforce the law in their own state, legislators in Charleston could do little to prevent out-of-state corporations from calling on the services of this agency. Indeed, even before the end of the West Virginia coal strikes, mine officials from the Colorado Fuel and Iron Company and other mining concerns in southern Colorado arranged for the importation of this agency's guards. Closely allied to that state's northern coal producers, who utilized the services offered by this agency in April of 1910, they were familiar with the reputation of the Baldwin-Felts men.[123] Albert Felts later told congressional investigators that he brought sixteen of his men into the strike district nearly a year before the September 1913 walkout. The most vicious of these, including George Belcher, Walter Belk, A. W. Brown, G. E. Hunt, W. A. Porter, and R. L. Bradly, acted as military overseers.[124] By the time this dispute ended, they had supplied coal operators with at least seventy-five armed men. Local authorities deputized many, including Walter Belk and Albert Felts.[125] In all of the states his men had operated in, Felts told investigators, he had found only one sheriff who refused to deputize his

Fig. 1.10 Baldwin-Felts men killed or wounded during the 1912–13 strike. Top:
W. W. Phaup, wounded by strikers, and Robert Stringer, killed near the village of Pratt.
Bottom: J. E. Hines, killed by miners at Mucklow, and D. C. Slater, who died during
a shoot-out at Eskdale. From Howard B. Lee, *Bloodletting in Appalachia: The Story of
West Virginia's Four Major Mine Wars and Other Thrilling Incidents of Its Coal Fields*
(Morgantown: West Virginia University Press, 1969).

agents.[126] As these men brandished their weapons and rubbed shoulders with angry miners on the streets of Trinidad, Aguilar, Walsenburg, and other coal communities, it proved only a matter of time before the strike district erupted in a wave of violence. As they had in the hills of West Virginia, they not only spilled more blood, prompting the introduction of government troops and an inquiry which condemned their actions, but also enraged the miners, who eventually retaliated.

Veteran guards Belcher and Belk touched off better than a year of open warfare in August when they killed a union organizer, George Lippiatt, on the streets of Trinidad.[127] After exchanging heated words with the two detectives, Lippiatt secured a gun from union headquarters, reappeared, and dared them to repeat their threats. Witnesses disagreed as to who fired the first shot, but when the smoke cleared the union man lay in the street, his body pierced by six bullets. Lippiatt fired his weapon only once.[128]

The day of the strike call, more than nine thousand miners and their families came down from the company-owned towns. Abandoning their homes, they set up tent colonies in the mouths of the canyons near Walsenburg, Forbes, Ludlow, Rugby, and other smaller towns.[129] Backed by a large war chest, union officials shipped in tents from the West Virginia strike district, purchased large tracts of land for the homeless strikers, and vowed to fight to the end.[130] Familiar with their reputation as brutal strikebreakers, the men who gathered in these makeshift communities loathed the Baldwin-Felts men, convinced that they were "employed not as guards of company property, but as a guerilla band to 'clean out' the tent colonies."[131]

Once the war erupted, both sides armed themselves. While union leaders spent over seven thousand dollars for guns and ammunition, the Colorado Fuel and Iron Company invested nearly thirty thousand dollars.[132] With Albert Felts acting as an intermediary, it purchased four machine guns from the West Virginia Coal Operators' Association.[133] Two were mounted in an armored car, which striking miners called the "Death Special." Designed by Albert Felts and built at the Pueblo Steel plant of the Colorado Fuel and Iron Company, its sides were constructed of heavy steel plating, and a searchlight was positioned near the driver's seat.[134] Strikers first saw this machine three weeks after the strike began, when detectives escorted fifty miners to the Las Animas County jail.

Arrested for picketing, these men marched before the "Death Special," offering no resistence.[135]

Manned by Baldwin-Felts guards, the "Death Special" also played a significant role in an attack on a strikers' tent colony. On October 17, after miners and mine guards exchanged fire outside a make shift community outside Forbes, a relief force of deputies arrived in this vehicle. In a pouring rain Belk and Belcher raked the miners' tents with over six hundred rounds, killing one miner and wounding a young boy, Marco Zamboni.[136] Hit nine times in the legs and crippled for life, Zamboni later testified before a House committee whose members believed this attack was "unjustifiable from any standpoint."[137] Fortunately many of the miners had earlier fled to a stone house nearby, thus averting an even greater disaster.[138]

Like the miners from the Appalachian coal fields, the western miners made their employer's hired guns pay a heavy price for their brutality.

Fig. 1.11 The "Death Special," an armored automobile equipped with a machine gun and a searchlight. Pictured manned by six well-armed Baldwin-Felts guards, it was employed to intimidate strikers throughout out the coal fields of Colorado during the strike-laden year of 1913. *Report on the Colorado Strike Investigation*, 63rd Congress, 3rd Session, House of Representatives, No. 1630 (Washington: GPO, 1915).

A striker named Louis Zancanilli shot and killed Belcher—a marked man since the day he and Belk gunned down Gerald Lippiatt in late November, 1913—as he emerged from a drugstore.[139] Zancanilli's shot to the back of Belcher's head was well aimed, for the victim always wore a bullet-proof vest.[140] Ironically, Belcher died near the spot where he had killed Lippiatt three months earlier.[141]

On April 20, 1914, months of escalating violence culminated in one of the bloodiest events of the age of industrial violence: the Ludlow Massacre. When a Colorado guard unit launched an unprovoked attack upon a strikers' tent colony, three miners and scores of women and children died. Six months earlier, Governor Elias Ammons had called out the Colorado National Guard. Far from impartial, this unit proved little more than a tool of the mine operators. When recruits began melting away with the coming of spring, commanders turned to mine guards and those in the employ of the Baldwin-Felts Agency to fill its ranks.[142] Their presence outraged strikers, who complained bitterly to Governor Ammons.[143] While the role played by the guards brought in from West Virginia in this incident is unclear, evidence indicates that in the days after, they participated in a reign of terror within the strike district. Accompanied by men of the Colorado militia, they sacked the home of Frank Baynes, a local rancher who had offered shelter to women and children of the Ludlow tent colony the day before the attack. In the wreckage of his home he discovered a note which read: "This is to be your pay for harboring the union. Cut it out or we will call again." It was signed "B. F. and C. N. G.," which Baynes believed stood for "Baldwin-Felts" and "Colorado National Guard."[144]

The Ludlow tragedy turned Colorado into a battlefield, as strikers poured into the strike zone. Although the agency's participation in this strike was now over, as the majority of its men had returned to West Virginia, at least one Baldwin-Felts man stayed. The Rocky Mountain Fuel Company employed Walter Belk to direct its Vulcan and Hecla mine guards as they battled better than two hundred strikers.[145] A week after the Ludlow massacre, guerilla war finally came to an end when President Wilson ordered the U.S. Army into Colorado's coal fields. Even after the strike ended, Belk toured the coal communities in the "Death Special," accompanied by the state's attorney general, in an effort to scare the strikers into supporting indictments against union officials.[146]

When the UMWA decided to challenge the mine owners in southern West Virginia less than seven years later, once again the men of the Baldwin-Felts Agency antagonized the strikers and soon found themselves involved in another bloodbath. Violence erupted in the spring of 1920 when one of the largest coal producers in the region, the Red Jackett Coal Company, turned to the Baldwin-Felts Agency to remove miners residing in their Stone Mountain coal camp.[147] Tom Felts assigned this task to his two brothers, Albert and Lee, and a posse of ten guards who arrived in Matewan, the nearest railroad town, on May 19. Although they carried out their orders without incident, news of their action spread quickly. When they attempted to board the train back to Bluefield, the town mayor, Cabell Testerman, and the chief of police, Sid Hatfield, blocked their path. While the Baldwin-Felts men despised both, they particularly disliked Hatfield, who not only understood the miners but also enforced the law in a way that favored them. Frustrated by his intransigence, Tom Felts had gone so far as to offer him three hundred dollars a month for his loyalty.[148] When Hatfield informed Albert Felts that he held a warrant for his arrest, Felts responded by saying he had a warrant of his own and that the sheriff would have to return to Bluefield with the detectives. They exchanged more heated words, then suddenly gunfire. From places of concealment on either side of the street came a murderous fusillade. In the first volley, five guards fell. The miners killed two more as they tried to escape. In all, only five managed to save themselves.[149] Hatfield later told the *Philadelphia Public Ledger* that "it was a question of life or death for me," and that "it was all over in two minutes."[150] In addition to the Baldwin-Felts men, including Albert and Lee Felts, Mayor Testerman and two miners met their deaths in this shootout.[151]

That night, the miners celebrated over the dead bodies, firing their guns into their lifeless forms.[152] Although only twenty-six, Sid Hatfield became a nationally known figure. Newspapers pictured him pointing two pistols and dubbed him "Two Gun" Sid Hatfield. The UMW union did its part, producing a film of his exploits called "Smilin' Sid."[153] In the weeks after this incident, the push for unionization increased as thousands of miners flocked into one of thirty-four locals in the area.[154] On July 1, 1920, the union officially called a strike and moved to close the mines in southern West Virginia.[155]

In late January 1921, as the strike raged on, Sid Hatfield and twenty-two other defendants charged with the murder of the two younger Felts brothers and their men in Matewan appeared before a jury in Williamson, West Virginia. People from throughout the region flocked into this town to see the biggest trial in the history of the state. It began on an ominous note as a score of heavily armed Baldwin-Felts detectives appeared on the streets. Hundreds of armed miners also marched upon Williamson, vowing to protect the defendants. The trial did not begin until the judge ordered both sides to withdraw.[156] John McDowell, one of the guards

Fig. 1.12 The seven Baldwin-Felts men killed in the gun battle at Matewan in May 1920. Top row, left to right: C. T. Higgins and Albert and Lee Felts, brothers of one of the founders of the agency. Bottom row, left to right: C. B. Cunningham, A. J. Booher, E. C. Powell, and J. W. Ferguson. From Howard B. Lee, *Bloodletting in Appalachia: The Story of West Virginia's Four Major Mine Wars and Other Thrilling Incidents of Its Coal Fields* (Morgantown: West Virginia University Press, 1969).

who escaped the miners' wrath in Matewan by swimming the river to Kentucky, appeared on the stand first and told his version of the events of May 19.[157] In addition to refuting the guards' interpretation of these events, the miners' attorney painted a picture of a private army in the employ of an out-of-state coal producer, preying upon women and children. He closed by saying that it was time that taxpayers, not the Baldwin-Felts Agency, governed Mingo County.[158]

Although the proceedings in Williamson lasted nine weeks, the longest murder trial until that time in West Virginia, they proved a farce, for all who served on the jury understood that their safety depended upon a vote of "not guilty."[159] On March 21, 1921, Harold W. Houston, council for the defense, heard the jury return the verdict all expected.[160] Their decision enraged Tom Felts, who announced that he would spend his last "cent and the last atom" of his energy to secure Hatfield's punishment.[161] He would not have to wait long.

Fig. 1.13 Main Street, Matewan, West Virginia, where seven Baldwin-Felts guards met their demise at the hands of Sid Hatfield and a group of enraged miners. From Howard B. Lee, *Bloodletting in Appalachia: The Story of West Virginia's Four Major Mine Wars and Other Thrilling Incidents of Its Coal Fields* (Morgantown: West Virginia University Press, 1969).

Before that summer ended, Hatfield and his good friend and fellow defendant, Ed Chambers, lay dead, gunned down by thugs in the employ of the Baldwin-Felts Agency. In late July authorities ordered both men, along with thirty-five strikers, to appear in Welch, the McDowell County seat, on August 1, 1921, to explain their role in an attack upon the Mohawk coal camp two weeks after the Matewan affair. Before leaving for this small town, Hatfield told Fred Mooney of the UMWA that Tom Felts arranged for this trial in order to get his revenge and that Mooney would never see him again.[162] Although they had been guaranteed safe passage by the town sheriff, as Hatfield and Chambers walked up the courthouse steps accompanied by their wives, Bill Salter, one the of the Baldwin-Felts guards to escape Matewan, and two compatriots, C. E. Lively and Buster Pence, fired upon them. Having left their weapons in their hotel rooms, the two men stood little chance.

Indeed, it was all over in a matter of seconds. "When the battle ended, Hatfield, still wearing his smile, and Chambers were sprawled on the sidewalk, dead."[163] According to Mrs. Chambers, Lively placed a gun behind her husband's ear and fired the last shot even though she pleaded, "Don't shoot at him anymore, you have killed him now."[164] One of the women later reported that neither man had been armed, but that upon returning to the steps after being led off by the guards, she saw both men lying on the pavement clutching pistols.[165] Howard B. Lee, a historian of the coal wars and an acquaintance of Buster Pence, believed that Pence or his friend "planted" these weapons on his two victims. Years later, Lee claimed that when boasting of his bloody deeds, Pence often remarked: "Kill 'em with one gun, and hand 'em another one." Moreover, another guard told Lee that he fired his pistol against the walls of the steps in order to make it appear that Chambers and Hatfield were armed.[166] Although scores of people witnessed the attack, fear prevented them from testifying. Acquitted on the grounds of self-defense, the three gunmen walked free on December 17, 1921.[167] All along Lively proclaimed that it was "a case of self-defense pure and simple," and that he "regretted having to shoot either of these men."[168]

The assassinations of Hatfield and Chambers turned rebellion into open warfare. When the arrival of Federal troops in the late summer of 1920 failed to bring order, Governor Ephraim Morgan declared martial law the following spring. As the eviction of miners increased, union

Fig. 1.14 "Two Gun" Sid Hatfield, Matewan's chief of police, earned the respect of the miners and the hatred of Thomas Felts. Baldwin-Felts men gunned him down outside the courthouse in Welch, West Virginia, three months after the Matewan massacre. From Howard B. Lee, *Bloodletting in Appalachia: The Story of West Virginia's Four Major Mine Wars and Other Thrilling Incidents of Its Coal Fields* (Morgantown: West Virginia University Press, 1969).

membership jumped dramatically and violence continued unabated. For example, during an all-out battle known as the "Battle of Blair Mountain," state officials employed air power to bomb a column of thousands of armed strikers as they attempted to march through Logan, West Virginia, and on to where strikers first vented their wrath against the Baldwin-Felts guards—Mingo County. The events culminating in the West Virginia Mine War of 1920–21 overwhelmed the capacity of the Baldwin-Felts Agency. Indeed, one mine manager concluded that Tom Felts had "'lost his grip' in Mingo County," and at least one other operator signed up with the UMWA.[169] Moreover, coal operators came to rely less and less on the services provided by this agency after the U.S. Coal Commission and the Senate Committee on Education and Labor concluded its inquiries into this dispute.[170] The coal commissioner's recommendations that the "use of paid company guards" be abolished received the backing of not only union leaders but even coal operators.[171] Although he blamed both sides for the bloodshed, the chairman of the latter inquiry, William S. Kenyon, indirectly placed the lion's share of the responsibility for the outbreak of violence on the guard system, noting: "It is the duty of the State to protect the properties of the operators."[172] Rather than risk further negative publicity the mine operators turned to more institutionalized means to discipline their workers, including a state police system that had become more professional after its inception in 1919. Other owners forced their workers to sign "Yellow Dog" contracts.[173] Until 1917 the courts did not consider such "contracts" legally binding. When the Supreme Court's ruling in the Hitchman case reversed that tradition, coal operators began requiring miners to sign contracts that, under threat of dismissal, prohibited them from joining a union. The agency that once provided their clients with nearly complete control over their workers had passed its time. The death knell for the Baldwin-Felts Agency finally came in 1935, when the West Virginia legislature made the deputization of private guards illegal.[174]

Long before West Virginia lawmakers moved to ban the importation of armed guards, it had become apparent that the days of private police were numbered. In addition to anti-Pinkerton laws regulating the shipment of armed guards across state lines, public police began to usurp these mercenaries' function as they began to take on their modern form. Moreover, most businessmen were coming to realize that the introduction of

Pinkerton-like forces, even in isolated rural environments, resulted in bloodshed and public outrage. Well aware of their clients' need to find new ways to discipline their workers while escaping public scrutiny, anti-union entrepreneurs showed their ability to adapt to the wants of employers who no longer wanted or needed private police.

2

ARMIES OF STRIKEBREAKERS FOR HIRE

IN SPITE OF THE PUBLIC anger and "anti-Pinkerton" legislation that the Homestead debacle generated, as the conflict between employers and their workers continued unabated, anti-union specialists remained important allies of the business community. With the promise of great rewards, some armed guard suppliers found ways to circumvent state legislation regulating their behavior. By the dawn of the new century, however, an increasing number of employers whose workers had abandoned their posts turned to those anti-union entrepreneurs who specialized in providing strikebreakers. Having long demonstrated their skill in utilizing the ranks of the unemployed, or black workers, or even recent immigrants to break strikes, in this age of professionalization many managers found it more expedient to turn their problem over to a strikebreaking general who commanded an army of professional strikebreakers.

Such troops provided the besieged employer with an acceptable method of disciplining his workforce. Unlike armed guards, who, to much of the public, differed little from mercenaries hired by feudal lords, strikebreakers operated under the protection of two long-established American economic rights: the businessman's right to hire whomever he pleased and the working man's right to work. Symbols of American economic liberty, they were even regarded in some circles as heroes for standing up for American ideals. Indeed, while state legislatures outlawed the use of private police, lawmakers across the country upheld the right of the businessman to employ strikebreakers. In spite of their special standing, the arrival of such armies generally provoked strikers and, if bloodshed spilled into the streets, occasionally the wrath of the community.

It was as early as the strike-laden decade of the 1890s that Jack Whitehead implemented the idea of organizing an army of professional strikebreakers. Breaking numerous strikes in the steel-producing region of western Pennsylvania during that decade, he was the first to earn the title "King of the Strikebreakers." Born in Cincinnati, Ohio, shortly after the middle of the nineteenth century, his early years provided little indication that he would one day become the steel workers' most feared enemy. As a young man he moved to Pittsburgh, where he found work in the steel mills. He was a skilled iron puddler, roller, and heater, and most regarded him as one of the best mill hands in the district. Although he could neither read nor write, he was "a man of exhaustive knowledge in mill work, able to do anything himself, and to instruct others."[1] Once a union man, after a heated disagreement he left his local, vowing never to return. He then moved to Birmingham, Alabama, where he plied his craft in that city's steel mills. After the Amalgamated Association of Iron and Steel Workers shut down the Clinton Mills in 1891, he returned to Pittsburgh, where he began his career as a strikebreaker. Commanding forty highly skilled black steel workers, within ten days his army broke the strike. For his efforts he reportedly earned ten thousand dollars.

During the last decade of the nineteenth century he and his "Forty Thieves" battled the steel workers around Pittsburgh on a number of occasions. In most cases, shortly after their arrival, smoke poured from the stacks of the besieged plant, convincing strikers that their efforts were of little use. Reporters, including one who told readers of the *Independent* that he was "as devoid of human fear as any human can be," mythologized Whitehead's life. By 1901, the first King of the Strikebreakers announced his retirement.[2] By demonstrating that money could be made from breaking strikes, he spawned a host of imitators.

It was during the early twentieth century that the generals of these armies of strikebreakers, men like James A. Farley and Pearl Bergoff, dominated the unionbusting industry. Capturing the attention of the public, both Farley and Bergoff earned the title "King of the Strikebreakers." For a fee they supplied hundreds and on occasions even thousands of men to restart their clients' plants or at least make it appear that workers were returning to their posts. While some possessed the skills needed, just as commonly their ranks were made up of drifters, vagabonds, or men who were too old or too enfeebled to tend the machinery of modern industry.

In 1904, the muckraker B. T. Fredricks wrote of James Farley in *Leslie's Magazine:* "In no single case where he has responded and taken hold of capital's end of a fight with labor, has labor won the fight. That is his business. He is the boss strikebreaker."[3] Born in Malone, New York, in 1875, Farley left home at the age of fourteen and, after a succession of odd jobs, settled in New York City.[4] In 1895, he joined a strikebreaking army, "hardly knowing what I was doing," he later noted, blaming his journey into this sordid profession on a toothache and "too much cocaine."[5] Leading fifteen special officers and standing his post "through rocks, bullets and dynamite until his skull was laid open," according to the *New York Times,* he proved his valor.[6] Promoted to district captain, he directed more than two thousand strikebreakers and helped break a traction strike in Philadelphia later that year. Both strikes proved chaotic, for not only did a number of competing detective agencies supply replacement workers but inexperienced company officials assumed command of these men. From this experience he recognized that an expert strikebreaking general in charge of his own army could offer a more effective service.[7]

Farley opened his own detective agency in New York City in 1902.[8] In addition to regular detective work, he took on industrial cases, specializing in streetcar strikes. He could not have selected a better field or time. Not only did the unskilled nature of streetcar driving enable him to find recruits with little difficulty but, as trolley lines stretched out into the country in the early twentieth century, nearly every major city suffered a traction strike. It also required little investment capital as the commanders of these armies generally carried their offices "in their hats." Moreover, although many communities were at odds with their traction companies because of poor service and generally supportive of the local carmen, in the name of American economic values state lawmakers usually protected strikebreakers.[9] For example, while one could be arrested for addressing "any offensive, derisive or annoying words" to the men of such armies in New Hampshire, in Michigan, state law prohibited strikers from interfering with strikebreakers by means of "threats, intimidation or otherwise."[10] There were also reported cases in which local authorities who had expelled strikebreaking troops were overruled by federal courts. During the steel strike of 1919, for example, the mayor of Cleveland, Ohio, rescinded his threat to arrest all arriving strikebreakers after being faced with a federal injunction. Similarly, a New Jersey judicial decision, handed down in 1920, overturned a Jersey City ordinance prohibiting the importation of strikebreakers.[11] Not until Congress enacted the Byrnes Act in 1935 did the federal government attempt to control the industry.[12]

To besieged traction companies Farley proved himself a good ally. One year after he entered this line of work the *New York Tribune* bestowed upon him the title "King of the Strikebreakers."[13] Two years later, editors for the *St. Louis Globe-Democrat* believed that "the Amalgamated Association of Street Railway and Electric Employees would have been a mighty power but for Farley, the man who is the cause of most of its failures in strike episodes."[14] By that time he had crushed twenty strikes, including streetcar walkouts in Philadelphia, Scranton, Cleveland, Providence, and Richmond.[15] The key to ending these strikes was "to get the cars running and to keep them running," he told a writer for the *New York Times*.[16]

Farley first tested his mettle during the Providence, Rhode Island, streetcar strike of 1902. It was during this dispute that he "attained his present rank as a strikebreaking general with absolute power, superior even to the president of a company," one reporter believed.[17] His army failed to tame the strikers, however. The day the strike began, the *Evening Telegram* reported that amongst "the traveling public, sympathy is all with the [streetcar] men."[18] Not only did passengers feel a great loyalty to the motormen and conductors who often lived in their communities, the introduction of outside strikebreakers only galvanized their hatred for the company. Violence erupted on June 5, when millworkers, college students, and middle-class folks blockaded the tracks, showered passing streetcars with debris, and even shot at the cars.[19] The next day the *Providence Journal* described the riot in a front-page headline: "Streets filled with rioters; cars destroyed, motormen and conductors terrorized."[20]

Fig. 2.1 James A. Farley in 1905 at the height of his career as "King of the Strikebreakers." From *Public Opinion*, March 25, 1905.

After this incident Farley's men made their runs reluctantly and occasionally refused to leave the carbarns.[21] Early the following month, despite widespread public support, the exhausted streetcar men capitulated. The arrival of state militia units armed with Gatling guns and an increasing rate of arrests backed by harsh sentences dampened their enthusiasm.[22]

After a successful campaign against the carmen of Richmond, Virginia, the next year, Farley found his services in demand in the city where he began his career.[23] When the Amalgamated Association of Street and Electric Railway Employees of America began preparations for a strike against the New York City Interborough Rapid Transit Company in the fall of 1904, he mobilized his army and shipped it to that city. This group numbered sixty men and, according to its leader, there was not "a 'quitter' among them." Although they believed "Farley's Bunch" was a "strange crew, who blow together with all the four winds of heaven the moment there is trouble," writers for the *New York Times* noted that they were all experienced railroad men, each selected with "a special view to physical courage and staying qualities."[24]

Farley rarely experienced difficulty mobilizing such an army. He claimed to maintain a roster of thirty-five thousand experienced transit workers, seven or eight hundred of whom he was able to mobilize immediately. Whenever trouble erupts, he once boasted, "I will send for these men wherever they happen to be, and pay their fare to the strike center. I can reach them at a minute's notice at any time."[25] Although most of these men held regular full-time jobs, a special agreement between Farley and their employers enabled them to leave their positions for as long as they were needed.[26] Each highly skilled veteran received twenty to twenty-five dollars per day. This scale compared favorably to the two dollars earned daily by ordinary motormen and conductors. Rather than the good wages, however, it was the "spirit of adventure rather than anything else that actuat[ed] them," Farley explained.[27] Among these men numbered a handful of college students, two physicians, several football players, one circus performer, and, according to the *New York Times,* several union men who had "been sold out by their leaders and left high and dry after a strike was over."[28] To supplement his gathering army, Farley set up a recruiting station in New York City. Thousands of men thronged this building "until far into the night." Each carried a card bearing these instructions: "Call at No. Ten Dey Street, nine o'clock

Monday morning, one flight up. Bring this with you. Yours truly, James Farley." While he preferred to hire experienced streetcar crews, he told a *New York Times* reporter "courage and a strong skeleton is what I look for in selecting men."[29]

Although well prepared for the coming storm, at the last minute the general manager of the Interborough Rapid Transit Company, August Belmont, agreed to meet with union representatives. A leading figure in the New York Democratic party, he wanted to avoid a strike that might reflect badly upon his party in the weeks before the coming presidential election. Accepting his offer of three dollars for a ten-hour day, union leaders instructed their members to return to their cars.[30] Days later, the *New York Times* bestowed upon Farley the title "Captain of Industry," noting that he had "reduced strikebreaking to a beautiful and effective system."[31] With the strike threat over, he withdrew his army.

When negotiations with the carmen's union broke down less than six months later, once again, Farley's army of five thousand men "each knowing what he had to do, and with a fair knowledge of how to do it" poured into New York from all over the country. Keeping secret their route and their destination, Farley shipped four hundred experienced street railway workers from Chicago in early March.[32] Quartered in Philadelphia, he threw these men into action the morning the strike erupted.[33]

At his headquarters on Van Buren Street, under the watchful eye of armed guards, Farley once again enlisted local men. Included in this group was one writer who signed on as a conductor. He later told readers of *World's Work* that amongst his new colleagues he found: "A sprinkling of the upper grade of hoboes; a large number of cheap 'sports'—devil-may-care young fellows, whose ideal life seemed to be a week of work, a week of the Bowery." He also claimed to have met a number of workmen "with the strained look of a man long out of a job."

Rather than lofty ideologies about the rights of private property, it was money that motivated these men, he reported.[34] Some of the men hired locally earned good pay, although much less than what his battle-tested veteran leaders made. While station platform men and ticket choppers and agents made $2.50 a day and second-class conductors and guards received $3.00 per day, Farley paid motor men and engineers $3.50 per diem.[35] Many were happy for the opportunity to work. Farley charged his clients five dollars per diem for each man.[36] The Interborough housed these men in a large carbarn, the floor filled with "cots two feet wide, built up to last a week, placed side by side, which each man shared with another."[37] Their repair shop at 148th Street and Lenox Avenue also served as a barracks.[38] Farley provided this army with a hospital, commissary, and legal services.[39]

An hour after the strikers left their cars on March 7, Farley's men assumed the controls. From a back room in an office building he commanded his troops, working the phones and giving orders to a string of messenger boys.[40] Never leaving his post, he took complete control of the Interborough system. When a reporter asked a worker if August Belmont ran the line, he responded by inquiring: "who the ___ is Belmont, Farley's running this road."[41] In spite of his Herculean effort, not all went smoothly. In mid-March, for example, six hundred strikebreakers rioted, convinced that they had not been paid in full. Police reserves put an end to their demonstration.[42] When other members of his army complained to the press that they were never informed that they had been hired as strikebreakers, Farley jumped up on a box and announced: "You were not kidnapped and you did know that you were coming here to break a strike. The man who says that is not so, lies." The men went back to work.[43] A week earlier an inexperienced operator caused a wreck that resulted in countless injuries and one fatality.[44]

While Farley remained in his headquarters, his employees, like the reporter for *World's Work* who claimed that he faced "jeers, grimaces and shaking fists from all sides," confronted angry sympathizers.[45] From union men, who often boarded these cars and harangued them throughout their runs, Farley's men encountered even more offensive insults. Occasionally the carmen employed a conciliatory approach. One striker said to this same reporter: "I know you need the coin or you wouldn't be doing this. If you quit your job and come over to our hall we'll show you a good time, give you all the money you expected to make out of this, and pay your fare to the town you come from." That same morning three other men offered him money to abandon his post, he reported.[46]

Although the trains ran poorly, within four days this walkout came to an end. According to one reporter if it "had not been for him [Farley] the strike would still be in full swing, or the corporation would have capitulated."[47] The local union soon folded and more than 60 percent of the strikers lost their jobs.[48] Not only did Farley's men fill many of the vacated positions, they also received fifty cents more per day than the strikers who returned to their jobs.[49] For those who wanted only to go home, Farley paid their fare.[50] He could afford to do so. The *New York Times* reported that the Interborough paid him three hundred thousand dollars for breaking this strike.[51] Belmont achieved his objective, however. For years the Interborough remained an open shop system.[52]

While Farley earned his reputation breaking traction strikes, his army was involved in a variety of labor struggles, including the 1905 Chicago Teamsters' strike. One of the city's bloodiest labor disputes, it ended when the union surrendered after 106 days, during which fourteen people had perished and an additional thirty-one had been wounded. Frightened not only by the strikers' militancy, but also by the police department's inability to provide protection to the seven to eight thousand strikebreakers recruited to drive the cartage companies' wagons, management called on Farley shortly after the walkout began.[53]

His chief lieutenant, Frank Curry, arrived on the evening of May 1. Assuming command of this gathering army from a man by the name of Buckminster, of the Metropolitan Detective Agency of Chicago, Curry announced, "I want no police. They are only in the way. Give me plenty

Death Marks First Day of Big Traffic Tie-Up on the Subway and "L"

Man Killed by the Crush in Grand Central Station, When Thousands of Persons Were Attempting to Reach Their Uptown Homes.

ELEVATED TRAIN BEYOND CONTROL IN PERIL OF JUMPING HIGH CURVE

Neither Side Keeps Its Promises—Trains Not Run on Schedule Time. While on the Other Hand Systems Are Not Blocked.

ALL SURFACE ROADS ARE OVERWHELMED

Police on Guard at All Stations on Both Lines Prevent Serious Trouble, Although Violence Is Threatened Often—Mayor Offers to Act as Mediator.

Many Injured in Rear End Crash

Inexperienced Motorman Said To Be Responsible for Fatal Accident in the Subway

THREE MAY DIE FROM INJURIES RECEIVED

BOY CHOPS FATHER FROM THE WRECK

Fire in the Garden Causes $50,000 Loss

Great Madison Square Structure Imperilled by Flames at Midnight After Show Is Over.

EXPLOSIONS EXCITE PATRONS OF HOTELS IN VICINITY

DAMAGE CONFINED TO FEW EXHIBITS

Fig. 2.2 Although Farley claimed his men were experienced streetcar operators, a fatal accident during the 1905 strike in New York led many to fear their employment. From the *New York Herald*, March 8, 1905.

of men and plenty of clubs." He then loaded three hundred of his men onto wagons and begun a tour of downtown.[54] Thus began "Curry's parade," the bloodiest incident of the strike. In addition to heavy loaded hickory canes, his men were armed with guns, knives, and razors. The *Chicago American* believed some were "veritable walking arsenals."[55] Curry planned to arm his men with Winchesters, and a number were so equipped, but an alarmed city council ended this effort.[56] That morning a brief melee ensued when, on their second circuit of the city, thousands of strikers and their sympathizers confronted them. The angry crowd outnumbered these ruffians and soon had them on the run. Those able to flee took shelter in a cold storage house. Curry eventually dropped out of the dispute, handing the reins back over to Buckminster. He later returned to St. Louis, ending his employer's participation in this strike.[57] Farley reportedly earned fifty thousand dollars for his efforts in Chicago.[58]

Although his army had been mauled in Chicago, after a string of successes in other cities Farley became a national figure.[59] Editors referred to him as "the best known strikebreaker in the United States" and "the best hated man in this country."[60] After he defeated the New York carmen his life became legendary to a fascinated public. Rumors circulated, for instance, that he paid a hundred-dollar bonus to any conductor who rode the first trolley out of the carbarn with him. His hometown newspaper contributed to his growing stature, reporting that he was "absolutely without fear" and "his methods" even "compel the admiration of his enemies."[61] Editors for *Public Opinion* joined in the adulation, telling their readers that he carried two bullets in his body. The *New York Herald* mentioned only one.[62] Although most lauded the exploits of the King of the Strikebreakers, John Graig, writing for *Collier's Weekly*, reported that a number of Farley's associates believed him a coward, for he offered little resistance on the more than one occasion when they robbed him of large sums of money.[63]

As the best-known strikebreaker in the country Farley became richer than "he had ever dreamed of being."[64] Doing more than ten million dollars' worth of business by 1914, he was able to pay his assistants, Frank Curry and a man named Wendell, handsomely.[65] Much of this income he earned from retainer work, as employers, including the New York Interborough, which awarded him one thousand dollars a day for two

Fig. 2.3 Frank Curry, Farley's chief lieutenant, who also reaped a fortune breaking strikes. From *World's Work,* July 1905.

months preceding the 1905 strike, paid him for the privilege of first or second call on his services.[66] Away from his rough-and-tumble business he lived the life of a country gentleman. He owned a fine home in Plattsburgh, New York, which he purchased from the Paul Smith Hotel Company in 1906.[67] He invested over twenty thousand dollars renovating this building. His home became the social center of that community, and Farley hosted extravagant parties in the huge dining rooms of the former hotel. Those lucky enough to receive an invitation included local and even national dignitaries.[68] Farley also owned fourteen horses and spent much of his free time on the trotting circuit.[69]

The San Francisco streetcar strike of 1907, one of the bloodiest disputes of the early twentieth century, brought Farley his greatest rewards. Rumors circulated that he earned one million dollars for his efforts in that city.[70] The strike began in early May, when two thousand members of the Amalgamated Association of Street and Electric Railway Employees of America, better known as the Carmen's Union, threatened to abandon their cars unless United Railways granted them a three-dollar wage for an eight-hour day.[71] The president of United Railways, Patrick Calhoun, rejected the carmen's demands and insisted that they abide by their contract of 1905.[72] He was convinced that he could break any strike proposed by the carmen, and events proved him correct.

Well before the carmen left their posts, Calhoun contracted with Farley, who agreed to bring four hundred strikebreakers into San Francisco. Their agreement stipulated that they would remain on the job until August 1.[73] Under contract with the Interborough Transit Company of Brooklyn, at that time Farley shipped these men by train to the west coast. One writer, who bragged that he had "seen many tough men," claimed to have never viewed "any others to equal the train load [Farley] shipped out of New York." When engine trouble sidetracked this train in the Badlands, these men descended upon a small town, which became "the scene of a raging battle," he reported. By nightfall, this group "had chased all the local bad men to the tall timbers."[74] The carmen of San Francisco were well acquainted with Farley and his army of ruffians. Three years earlier, they abruptly ended a threatened strike and agreed to an unsatisfactory contract once they discovered that Calhoun contracted with this strikebreaker to bring in more than three hundred well-armed men. They also remembered his boast that he would "make the malcontents know that the cars are going to run, and that anybody who gets in the way is going to be hurt."[75]

When Richard Cornelius, president of the carmen's union, announced that members would walk out on May 5, Calhoun gave the men two days to return to their posts.[76] In the meantime, Farley's army arrived from the east.[77] Calhoun housed these men in United Railway's carbarns. Anticipating a long siege, he converted the barns into arsenals and surrounded each with a barbed wire fence.[78] Although the electric lights in these huge buildings burned all day long to prevent thievery, according to a writer who secured a position with United Railways, "life in the barns [was] by no means a hard one," for the company provided for all their needs.[79] As thousands gathered to see this army file into the barns, United Railways made no effort to operate the cars and averted bloodshed on the first day.[80]

Fig. 2.4 Strikebreaking made Farley a wealthy man. Purchased in 1906, his home in Plattsburgh had once been a hotel. Courtesy Special Collections, Feinberg Library, Plattsburgh State University.

The following day, however, came to be known as "Bloody Tuesday." Violence erupted when Calhoun ordered Farley's men to take out six cars. At 3:25 P.M. the first group left the main barn and began their trip down Filmore Street to Market Street. Each operator wore the uniform of a United Railways car inspector and carried a revolver.[81] Between three and five thousand strikers and sympathizers quickly surrounded these vehicles, hurling rocks and bricks. As the windows shattered, the anxious strikebreakers fired into the crowd. From inside the barn the remainder of Farley's men and a contingent of private detectives also opened fire.[82] An Associated Press reporter who rode on horseback behind the cars reported that a guard on the rear platform of the lead vehicle fired the first shot, striking a man in the arm. This shooting, the *New York Times* reported, "aroused the mob to a frenzy." Running down Turk Street in pursuit of the cars, they showered them with stones and bricks as Farley's men repeatedly fired upon them.[83] This melee left twenty-five people dying or seriously wounded.

Although the middle-class citizenry of San Francisco undoubtedly upheld the right of the strikebreaker to work and the employer's right to hire whomever he desired, the outbreak of violence on May 7 swung public opinion against Calhoun and the United Railways. As President Cornelius of the Carmen's Union rallied the people of San Francisco to the support of the strikers, editors for the *San Francisco Chronicle* denounced the shooting as wanton massacre by imported gunmen.[84] The next day, the chief of police announced that he would arm his men with rifles and, he asserted, "if any strikebreakers start shooting from the cars they will be shot in return by the police."[85] Earlier he ordered the strikebreakers to disarm, and his men arrested the thirteen members of Farley's army whom they believed fired into the crowd on the second day of the strike.[86] Later released on bail furnished by United Railways, they charged that the police beat them and deprived them of food and water while incarcerated.[87]

While they may have mistreated Farley's men, local authorities were far from the strikers' loyal allies. To these men the businessman's right to hire whomever he desired remained important. Although the police chief promised that his men would never guard or operate the trolleys, twenty-one strikebreakers took out two cars flanked by a patrol of twenty officers days after the shooting.[88] Throughout the spring and early summer of 1907, the cars made their runs, manned by "Farleyites," who openly wore their revolvers. Within one week of the onset of the strike, one hundred vehicles were in operation, many accompanied by a well-armed police guard.[89]

In spite of this protection, nearly every day skirmishes erupted as strikers and sympathizers threw bricks and even fired at these vehicles. On May 25, for instance, they stoned a number of cars and later placed obstructions on the tracks.[90] Although the carmen were losing the battle, for months no Farleyman dared to venture out of the barns at night.[91]

Fig. 2.5 An injured strikebreaker receives help during the 1907 San Francisco streetcar strike. On May 7, "Bloody Tuesday," strikers and their supporters used an assortment of projectiles to stop Farley's armed trolley drivers from leaving the barns. Walter P. Reuther Library, Wayne State University.

In early June, one lost his life when he opened fire on a crowd.[92] By the beginning of the next month it became obvious that the Carmen's Union was engaged in a losing battle: editors for the *Argonaut* told their readers, "The street car strike is looking for a place to fall."[93] After the violence of the first couple of weeks of the strike, Calhoun and the United Railways made steady progress toward restoration of normal service. By early August, he enlisted enough permanent replacements to enable Farley's men to return to the east.[94] Their services were needed in Philadelphia as that city's streetcar operators threatened to go out on strike.[95]

Managers like Patrick Calhoun found an able ally in James Farley. Indeed, in a career spanning ten years, Farley claimed not to have lost any of his thirty-five strike jobs.[96] Whereas anxious businessmen regarded Farley's men as a godsend, to a middle class angered by labor's militancy and the contempt it showed for the rights of private property they were an accepted part of the struggle between workers and their employers. When strikebreakers' presence precipitated violence, however, ordinary citizens were apt to change this view.[97]

As the first decade of the twentieth century came to a close, so too did Farley's days of fame as the reigning King of the Strikebreakers. Suffering from tuberculosis, he rejected the job of breaking a streetcar strike in Philadelphia in 1910. Too weak to take up this battle, he claimed to have turned this job down because "the strikers were in the right."[98] In September of 1913, the *New York Times* reported that he spent his last days surrounded by a guard of ten men, watching the races at the Empire City Track in Yonkers. "'My horses are all I have to live for now,'" he reportedly claimed as he lay dying.[99] On September 11, 1913, he finally passed away in his home in Plattsburgh, New York. He was only thirty-nine years old.[100] This lucrative field now lay open for those who had long coveted his title.

Among the dozens of strikebreaking entrepreneurs who stood ready to inherit the title "King of the Strikebreakers" were men like John "Black Jack" Jerome, who helped bring the Denver Tramway strike of 1920 to an end, R. J. Coach of the Coach Detective Agency of Cleveland, Ohio, and Archie Mahon and James Waddell of the Waddell and Mahon Agency.[101] One contender, Pearl Louis Bergoff, stood above all of these men. At the end of his career he could claim that while others "may break a buttonhole makers' strike . . . when it is steel or utilities or railroads they come to me. I'm dean—been at it thirty years and made millions breaking strikes in this country."[102] Although he was prone to exaggeration and self-promotion, this proved no idle boast. Sending his army against workers in more than three hundred strikes, some of them the largest and bloodiest labor disputes of the time, he became the most important strikebreaker of the twentieth century.[103]

While Whitehead and Farley pioneered this form of unionbusting, Bergoff took it to a new level. Under his reign anti-union services became, if not more refined, at least more professional and businesslike. His agency acted like any subcontractor rather than a loosely organized army of ruffians. He not only joined in written contracts with his clients, employed a sales staff, and developed a command structure, he expected "to take care of everything from toothpicks in the commissary to the general managership" of a strike.[104] When frightened businessmen enlisted his services they turned to a specialist in labor control who claimed never to have "steered them wrong."[105] As America's most important strikebreaking general, he also developed a national notoriety, as editors devoted considerable space to his activities and often sought out his advice on industrial matters.

Bergoff was born in Detroit, Michigan, in the early spring of 1876. His father's occupation as a land speculator kept the family on the move, and by his seventh birthday his family had packed their possessions and moved nearly twenty times, finally settling in the Dakota Territory. During his early years in the Dakotas Bergoff was a self-admitted source of numerous complaints from the neighbors. It was no wonder that the future King of the Strikebreakers proved more than a handful. He loathed his feminine name and the curly red hair his mother so adored. A year after she passed away, his father severed all ties to his eldest son, dropping him off in Chicago and telling him to find his own way. The young Bergoff worked as a newsboy on the Baltimore and Ohio Railroad for two years and later as a cabin boy on a Great Lakes vessel. He eventually moved back to Michigan, hiring on the Sault Sainte Marie Railroad as a section hand. Tiring of that job, he headed east, landing in New York City in 1894.

There he began his career as a detective, working for the Brooklyn Heights Railroad and the Metropolitan Street Railway in Manhattan as a spotter. In that capacity he rode the trolley lines making sure the conductors recorded all the fares they accepted. He later worked for an investment firm as a tracer, tracking down debtors, and for a number of detective agencies specializing in domestic cases.[106] At some point, James A. Farley, whom Bergoff later described as a "kingpin among strikebreakers," provided him with work.[107]

After nearly ten years of plying his trade for others, in 1905 he formed his own detective agency, the Vigilant Detective Agency of New York. "Money is my sole aim," he stated as he began offering personal protection services to wealthy New Yorkers.[108] Two years later, joining forces with his three brothers and changing the name of their firm to Bergoff Brothers Strike Service and Labor Adjusters, he entered into the growing field of labor relations.[109] In a newspaper interview years later, he recalled that he decided to join the strikebreaking profession because "there was more money in industrial work."[110] Events proved Bergoff correct. From the end of the depression of 1907 until the early 1920s, the Bergoff brothers enjoyed one banner year after another.

Although he would come to be an important and trusted ally within the business community, Bergoff's first efforts at strikebreaking would hardly have earned him a reputation as a formidable ally. During the New York City garbage cart drivers' strike of 1907, for example, he supplied that city's street-cleaning commissioner with three hundred men, many of whom fled their posts upon arrival. Strikers and their sympathizers intimidated the remainder. On June 28, for instance, a well-armed group surrounded forty of these men and forced them to return to the stables.[111] When city officials convinced them to leave the safety of the barns, strikers pelted them and their police escorts with rocks, bottles, and bricks from the tenement rooftops. On a number of occasions, city officials called in reserve units to rescue these men.[112] The next day little changed. The *Evening World* observed that before "great throngs of Italians [strikers] the strikebreakers were . . . trembling with apprehension."[113] Adding to the city's problems, nearly fifty "volunteers" from the Health Department refused to work beside Bergoff's strikebreakers.[114] In the waning days of the strike, the situation deteriorated further when Bergoff brought in a group of black strikebreakers. The *New York Herald* believed that their deployment resulted in "one of the fiercest riots in the history of San Juan Hill." This tumult marked the end of the walkout.[115] On July 1, the strikers agreed to return to their carts. The City of

Fig. 2.6 Pearl L. Bergoff at the time of the bloody Pressed Steel Car Strike of 1909. After Farley passed away, Bergoff assumed the throne of the "King of the Strikebreakers." From Edward Levinson, *I Break Strikes! The Technique of Pearl L. Bergoff* (New York: Robert M. McBride and Company, 1935; rpt., New York: Arno and New York Times, 1969).

New York paid Berghoff more than twenty-four thousand dollars for the services of his army.[116]

Many of the contracts they won during their heyday, including an order to end a walkout at the Pressed Steel Car Company of McKees Rocks, Pennsylvania, in the summer of 1909, proved terribly violent. The elder Bergoff described this dispute as the bloodiest strike he had ever seen.[117] The walkout began on July 13, when forty men refused to return to their posts until management made clear its method of payment. (Earlier, the company had introduced a wage-scale system which lumped workers into pools and made their earnings dependent upon the production of their group.) When the company fired the forty men, six hundred of their colleagues laid down their tools. The next day, all but five hundred joined the strike.[118] In the end, as many as eight thousand employees representing sixteen nationalities took part in the bitter upheaval. Under the leadership of the radical Industrial Workers of the World (IWW), the strikers held out for nearly three months.[119] While American economic principles generally offered strikebreaking troops protection, this strike demonstrates that laissez-faire principles occasionally gave way to a public that could not stand by while outside forces instigated violence.

Shortly after the walkout began, plant manager James Rider contracted with the Bergoff brothers, who agreed to "produce promptly . . . a total of five hundred able bodied workmen" as well as guards to "assist in any capacity about our shops and act as guards day and night." Rider promised to pay five dollars per man supplied and to furnish these men with "rough sleeping quarters, to consist of cots, blankets and pillows within the plant closure."[120] From Philadelphia, where he recently helped to break a traction dispute, Bergoff set the McKees Rocks recruiting campaign in motion.

The army he gathered was organized into a military-like chain of command. In charge were the captains. Permanent employees, they assembled the recruits, made out the payroll, and strategically positioned the men. The lieutenants—or as they were known in strikebreaker parlance, the nobles—acted as guards and front line leaders, shielding the rank and file from angry strikers. Bergoff estimated that his agency generally supplied one guard for every fifteen or twenty strikebreakers.[121] Often, these men were armed and deputized as police officers. "We have a tentative understanding with local sheriffs, as has any large agency like ours that knows its business," he once claimed.[122] Setting up a recruiting headquarters in a basement office on West 33rd Street in New York, his brother, Leo, filled his quota of guards with men from the Bowery within hours. Such a rough-and-tumble stream of men pushed in and out of this office that the owner believed her renters had opened "a gambling establishment."[123]

On the bottom rung of his army could be found the foot soldiers, commonly known as finks. While some accepted these jobs because they were too incompetent or old to find employment, many were shiftless men who "don't really want work . . . what they want is excitement and easy money."[124] Many others, the *New York Times* reported, were shipped "direct to McKees Rocks from immigrant vessels without realizing that they were to assume the part of strikebreakers and without understanding . . . what perils they would encounter."[125] Fred Reiger, a German immigrant, who told a governmental inquiry that he and five other men answered an advertisement for "machinists" in a Manhattan newspaper, was among those recruited in New York. They appeared at 205 West 33rd Street, where they met Leo Bergoff and Sam Cohen, who informed them that they planned to hire "'1,600 railroad car builders.'"[126] Cohen and the younger Bergoff shipped these men to the strike zone in boxcars. After two days without any food, Reiger and his fellow "machinists" found themselves in the yards of the Pressed Steel Car Company.[127] For the next nine days they slept, ate, and worked in a large barn with two thousand other men. Their meals consisted of cabbage and bread.[128]

Shortly after the walkout began, violence erupted outside the plant as strikers greeted the trainloads of strikebreakers with rocks, bottles, and other debris. Inside the compound, a second battle broke out hours later when terrified strikebreakers demanded that guards escort them out of the stockade.[129] Later that same day, the major battle of this strike took place when a company-owned vessel, the *Steel Queen*, crossed the Ohio River and attempted to land 350 strikebreakers. Met by an equal number of strikers, the *Steel Queen* made for the opposite shore after the two sides exchanged more than one hundred shots.[130] Although strikers won the Battle of the Ohio, throughout the next month Bergoff's men poured into the plant. On August 13, more than three hundred arrived on the *Steel Queen*. The next day one hundred more stepped off this vessel.[131]

Before this dispute ended, he managed to place twelve hundred men behind company fences.[132]

As new recruits continued to arrive, those trapped inside the compound began slipping out. One of these men, Albert Vamos, an Austro-Hungarian immigrant, significantly altered the direction of the dispute when he told the vice-consul for the Austro-Hungarian government, Edgar L. G. Prochnick, that he and others had been held against their will. Shocked by what he heard, Prochnick requested that the United States government investigate charges of "peonage" in the plant. Although earlier requests for such an inquiry met rejection, by late August an official investigation was under way.[133] During these hearings Federal District Attorney John H. Jordan heard countless men testify that Bergoff's lieutenants lured them to McKees Rocks under false pretenses, paid them less than promised, and provided them with tainted food.[134] Many claimed that the guards not only mistreated them but forcibly detained them; one recruit told the committee, "Any place you wanted to go you would be questioned . . . if they didn't like your answer, you would just get your head knocked off."[135]

The star witness, Nathaniel Shaw, directed many of his charges against "Big" Sam Cohen, the Bergoff brothers' right-hand man. Cohen, he claimed, surrounded himself with thirty-five guards who intimidated and fleeced the strikebreakers. According to Bergoff, "On every big job there appears to be what are called musclemen" who "get at any graft that goes on when we are too busy to prevent it."[136] They often demanded a "rake-off" from the many crap games one could find going on, he went on to explain.[137] Indeed, Shaw testified that Cohen threatened to end their crap game unless he received a "rake-off."[138] Those who defied these plug-uglies found themselves in a boxcar prison. One of Shaw's fellow strikebreakers told investigators that this jail was "absolutely suffocating." He went on to explain: "They had us put in there, and there was no urinal, and they closed us up in that car."[139] Against these men the strikebreakers stood little chance. A *New York Times* reporter, describing Cohen as "huge in stature, weighing perhaps 240 pounds," wrote that when he asked Cohen, "How is it that you are so fond of beating people?" he responded sarcastically, "what, me beating people? Why, I wouldn't hurt a fly."[140] Although the strikebreakers seemed to relish the opportunity to tell their horror stories, when either one of the Bergoff brothers appeared in the courtroom, not one man spoke out against his treatment in the plant. Writers for the *New York Times* believed that they exerted a "strange unanalysable quality of mastership" over those men who testified against them.[141]

At the end of August, the tide turned against the Pressed Steel Car Company. In addition to the exposure of the conditions in the plant, the citizens of Pittsburgh and McKees Rocks were horrified when strikers and strikebreakers clashed on Sunday, August 22, in a bloody battle. As Bergoff's men returned to the plant early that evening, angry strikers blocked their path. When words and persuasion failed to convince their replacements to quit their posts, fists flew and both sides began shooting. By the end of the day, city officials counted six dead, six dying, and nearly fifty injured.[142] Local papers, generally sympathetic to the company, now called for an end to the strike and began expressing sympathy for the strikers.[143] Compounding the company's problems, Bergoff's mercenaries continued to flee the plant. For example, on August 28, sixty strikers who slipped into the plant as scab laborers easily persuaded nearly three hundred strikebreakers to come out with them.[144] During the first week in September, after days of open warfare, management finally acknowledged defeat by entering into negotiations with the strikers.[145] During the troubles at McKees Rocks, twenty-two people died, including two of Bergoff's men. He later told a reporter: "We paid four or five thousand dollars for each of our men killed. The income was so large that this expense made no difference."[146]

The debacle at McKees Rocks did little to hurt Bergoff's business. The next year proved one of his best as the Erie Railroad and the Chicago, Burlington, and Quincy Railroad called on his services.[147] Later that winter, when five thousand conductors and motor men called a strike against the Philadelphia Rapid Transit Company, he secured "one of the biggest jobs I handled."[148] Bergoff rarely experienced trouble finding enough men to fill his armies. "I can produce more manpower than any other man in the United States. I've had 10,000 men on my payroll," he once boasted to a reporter.[149] He kept track of his men with the aid of an extensive list, which included every man he ever employed, his address, and his training and experience. He once referred to this index system as "my priceless stock in trade; the core of my business."[150] When he needed additional men he spread the word where unemployed men gathered or called a charity employment agency or a flophouse.[151] Shortly after he pulled his army out of Philadelphia, he handled "a comparatively small job" for the Delaware and Hudson Railroad. Years later he boasted that not only had he earned thirty-five thousand dollars for his efforts, but the head of this railroad wrote him a personal letter thanking him for his "efficient service in breaking the strike." The next year brought work at the Baldwin Locomotive Works and a trip to New York to break a strike of that city's street sweepers. The latter dispute earned him another letter of recommendation. A strike along the pier in Boston, a hotel walkout in New York, and a dispute on the Lehigh Valley Railroad lines occupied his attention the next two years. During this period Bergoff assumed the title "Red Demon." This he claimed resulted from "my red hair and reputation in strikes." Although "I look gentle . . . when I'm directing 1,000 men in the midst of a mob of strikers, I'm a different man," he went on to explain.[152] In 1913, executives called upon the Red Demon to break a strike of telegraph operators on the Missouri, Kansas, and Texas Railroad. Other clients that year included the Erie Railroad and the Philadelphia and Reading Railroad.[153]

In the years before World War I, Bergoff and other men who supplied employers with armies of strikebreakers prospered in an environment in which their tactics were often lauded by the middle class as justifiable excesses in the defense of the rights of free enterprise. However, with bloodshed often the end result of their introduction and as the well-worn concepts of a laissez-faire economy gave way to a growing sense of social responsibility, an examination of the role such forces played in the struggle between employer and employee became inevitable. Established two decades after the Homestead inquiries, the Commission on Industrial Relations (CIR) provided a sweeping denunciation of this form of strikebreaking.[154] After fifty-four days of hearings during which the commission heard from five hundred witnesses, on June 15, 1915, the CIR released its report.[155] The majority of commissioners deemed the activities of anti-union mercenaries a contributing element in the "Denial of Justice," one of the four factors they listed as leading to industrial violence.[156] Moreover they challenged those economic beliefs that protected strikebreakers. For example, they pointed out that the long-held axiom guaranteeing a man's right to work "seems to be based on the conception that the strikebreaker is normally a working man who seeks work and desires to take the place of a striker." Almost without exception, they argued, "the strikebreaker is not a genuine workingman but is a professional who merely fills the place of a worker and is unable or unwilling to do steady work, or, if he is a bonafide workingman, that he is ignorant of conditions or compelled to work under duress."[157] They also questioned the sacred doctrine of the businessman's "right to do business," arguing that the prerogatives of business may be restricted "whenever it is dangerous or in any way deleterious to the public."[158] In their recommendations for quieter industrial relations a number of the commissioners called for legislation regulating private detective agencies (strikebreaking agencies) in order to "insure the character of their employees and limit their activities to the 'bona fide' business of detecting crime."[159]

There can be little doubt that the CIR failed in its mission. Beset by discord, the commission lacked the unanimity required for congressional enactment of its legislative proposals. World War I further submerged public interest so that by Armistice Day few remained interested in its work.[160] Operating in a climate unreceptive to labor's needs, they would have to wait until a more enlightened time for their views to gain acceptance. Legally unencumbered, the anti-union operator remained free to practice his trade.

As the CIR called witness after witness to the stand, Bergoff never slowed his operation. The year the commission released its final report he joined forces with James Waddell of the Waddell and Mahon Agency. A national strikebreaking firm with offices in Philadelphia, Boston, Baltimore, and Chicago, its officers could boast of breaking dozens of strikes, including a bloody copper miners' walkout at the Calumet and Hecla mines during the winter of 1913–14.[161] Shortly after this dispute ended in April 1914, Archie Mahon passed away. Unable to carry on alone, Waddell joined forces with the Bergoff brothers. While the elder Bergoff assumed the presidency of the firm of Bergoff Brothers and Waddell, Waddell took charge of field operations.[162]

When workers at the Bayonne plant of the Standard Oil Company of New Jersey began a weeklong strike in the middle of June 1915, Bergoff and his new partner secured one of their first big jobs.[163] Standard executives were well acquainted with Bergoff. Two years before the refinery workers walked away from their posts, the Red Demon brought into

Bayonne a small army of men who quickly ended a strike at the Herman Brothers' Company, a local cap-making concern.[164] Bergoff was also a leading member of that community, settling there in 1909 with his young wife of two years. She disapproved of his profession as well as his friends and had urged him to move from New York City. Financed by the fortune he made from breaking strikes, he took on the appearance of a successful businessman in his adopted city. He built a three-story, sixteen-room mansion in the fashionable part of town and employed servants, a chauffeur, and a part-time gardener. Developing a small tract of modestly priced homes and later erecting the Bergoff Building, a four-story office building, he became known as a building contractor. Appearing at social gatherings with town leaders, he quickly ingratiated himself to the community's elite. He contributed to both the Democratic and Republican parties, and at one time awarded nine rooms in his building to the Red Cross.[165] In 1916 the firm of Bergoff Brothers and Waddell

Fig. 2.7   One of the founders of the Waddell and Mahon Agency, James Waddell joined forces with Bergoff to form Bergoff Brothers and Waddell in 1915. From *American Magazine,* January 1917.

donated twenty-five hundred dollars to the Red Cross, leading the agency's list of contributors for that year.[166]

Although the Standard Oil Company awarded Bergoff Brothers and Waddell nearly two hundred thousand dollars for their efforts during the refinery dispute, rather than cowing the refinery workers into submission, Bergoff's men had only inflamed them. After five days, the town resembled an armed camp, and no fewer than five strikers had met their deaths. When another strike broke out at this same refinery months later, Standard managers did not call upon the services of Bergoff and his partners.[167]

A few months after they pulled their troops out of Bayonne, Bergoff Brothers and Waddell answered the Wilkes-Barre Railway Corporation's call for help when their motor men and conductors issued a strike call on October 14, 1915.[168] To calm management's fears that outsiders would provoke violence, Waddell agreed to take personal charge of this

Fig. 2.8 The Standard Oil strike of 1915. Bergoff Brothers and Waddell's first major strike job proved disastrous as four strikers perished. Armed with handguns, the strikers stood little chance against Bergoff's men, who carried Winchesters. From Edward Levinson, *I Break Strikes! The Technique of Pearl L. Bergoff* (New York: Robert M. McBride and Company, 1935; rpt., New York: Arno and New York Times, 1969).

strikebreaking operation. First, in order to avoid the accidents that so often accompanied streetcar strikes, he hired 250 experienced conductors and operators laid off from the Coney Island and Brooklyn Railroads.[169] Shipping these recruits over the Lehigh Valley Railroad and unloading them onto a spur track which ran onto company property, he avoided the violence that usually followed the arrival of such troops into a strike zone.[170] Taking charge of training those men hired locally, he taught them the basic mechanics of the equipment by dismantling one car. He also laid a short section of track on company property where they gained experience operating the cars. His efforts proved successful. No serious accidents were charged to inexperienced operators during this dispute.[171]

In spite of occasional skirmishes between strikers and Bergoff and Waddell's men, including one incident in which an angry crowd of three hundred strikers attacked two strikebreakers, kicking them until "they begged for mercy," the latter eventually opened and then ran the lines until the Wilkes-Barre company hired enough recruits to take over.[172] Once Waddell had trained enough of these men, his battle-hardened veterans either moved to another line or left the city. By the beginning of March, 1916, he had reduced his army to 110 men. Two weeks later he handed over to traction officials the last two lines.[173] With the help of these mercenaries, the Wilkes-Barre Railway Corporation was able to operate its cars during the first critical months of the strike. Slowly it wore the union down. Forced to the bargaining table, the strikers conceded on nearly every point.[174]

After defeating striking carmen in Wilkes-Barre and trolley crews on the New York Interborough lines the next year, earning $204,000, Bergoff Brothers and Waddell suffered a major setback in Kansas City in the summer of 1917.[175] Leo C. Bergoff and one of his lieutenants, J. C. Troy, arrived in this Midwestern town on August eighth of that year.[176] That evening at the Hotel Baltimore, where he made his headquarters, the younger Bergoff told a reporter for the *Kansas City Post,* "We got a contract to run the streetcar system of this city and we'll not only run it, but we'll break the strike." He went on to boast: "Why we've broken strikes where 25,000 men were out, and we only have a little strike here with 2,000 men out. A cinch I say."[177] In spite of his promises the situation quickly deteriorated once his men arrived. On August 11 strikers and sympathetic townsmen besieged Bergoff's army of seven hundred strikebreakers as they were moved to the carbarns. When the crowd braved the police and blocked their path, "the 'finks' scattered by way of all available streets and alleys." According to the editor of the *Kansas City Star* "the rout was complete."[178] Three days after his arrival, while an angry crowd searched in vain for Bergoff, thousands of strikers and sympathizers marched what remained of his army to Union Station, where they forced these men to board a train out of town.[179] Less than a week after it began, the Kansas City Streetcar Strike came to an end.[180]

In spite of their retreat in Kansas City, the increasing strike activity of the postwar years brought Bergoff Brothers and Waddell more work. In 1920, the agency helped to end the Erie Railroad switchmen's walkout by supplying railroad officials with thousands of strikebreakers. Bergoff boasted that he grossed two million dollars on this job.[181] Later they

Fig. 2.9 Days after his brother promised to end the Kansas City Streetcar Strike, Bergoff's army's humiliating retreat from that town is reported in front-page headlines.

brought three thousand strikebreakers into New York City four days after the Brooklyn Rapid Transit (BRT) strike began.[182] BRT officials paid Bergoff Brothers and Waddell $712,000, prompting the mayor to launch a "special and exhaustive inquiry."[183]

While the postwar decade began well for Bergoff Brothers and Waddell, opportunities quickly vanished with the prosperity of the Coolidge years and the labor peace that followed. Although workers erupted in a number of bloody strikes in the South, the number of labor disputes fell by more than 50 percent overall.[184] More important, the business community could not help but be aware that while labor's house declined from five million strong to less than three and a half million, they basked in the public's growing reverence for the material accomplishments of the age. The postwar period also brought subtle changes in the relationship between capital and labor as employers adopted even more sophisticated forms of union control, including welfare-capital schemes. Exercising greater control over their employees, the business community had fewer reasons to pay the high costs of the professional strikebreaker. Indeed, from 1924 until 1934, Bergoff and others found little work.[185] He once complained "business got so goddamn lousy I closed the office in 1925 and went to Florida."[186] His ten-year reign as the King of the Strikebreakers provided him with plenty of money to invest in that state's land boom. By the time the paper boom collapsed and the hurricane of 1925 finished off the Florida real estate market, he had lost more than two million dollars.[187] Within two years he returned to New York City and once again began building homes.[188] He would soon find his strikebreaking services in demand.

While the strike, according to Irving Bernstein, "had fallen into almost total disuse" during the 1920s, workers quickly rediscovered its utility as the nation slipped into the worst depression in history. In 1932 alone, 325,000 workers walked away from their posts. This figure increased to more than one million the next year and then jumped by another half million the following year.[189] As these numbers continued to increase, the business community's growing fear provided Bergoff with an opportunity to regain his fortune and his title. Indeed, he told one reporter, "I can see so much strife ahead I don't know which way to turn."[190] Not only did employers feel increasingly besieged by their workers, as a number of the nation's lawmakers came to sympathize with the cause of organized labor and as the public's reverence for the businessman waned with the Great Depression, many managers believed that they had been forsaken by those who once stood behind them.

During the Depression years Bergoff and his brothers operated out of four rooms in the Fred F. French building at 551 Fifth Avenue in New York City. On the eleventh floor could be found two of his companies: the Bergoff Detective Service Company, a licensed detective agency, and the Bergoff Service Bureau. The latter firm specialized in strikebreaking.[191]

As the nation slipped into economic doldrums the onetime King of the Strikebreakers joined forces with another strikebreaker, Nat Shaw, to bring the Standard Oil truck drivers' strike to a premature end. Although the activities of their men, including one who was arrested for carrying a

Fig. 2.10 Although his heyday was coming to an end, Pearl L. Bergoff remained confident that the increasing levels of strike violence spawned by the Depression would provide him the opportunity to earn his title back. Photograph for *Fortune* by Aitkins ©1935 Time, Inc. All rights reserved.

machine gun through the streets of Brooklyn, prompted Police Commissioner Grover Whalen to insist that the oil companies "cease using guerrillas," they earned $175,000 for less than a month's effort.[192] Even though the next two years brought Bergoff little work, by 1933 business began to improve, and he earned fifty thousand dollars that year. The next year he doubled that figure.[193]

Bergoff's luck eventually ran out, as his firm faced one setback after another. A squabble over the division of spoils from the truck drivers' strike ended his partnership with Shaw. Then when workers in San Francisco erupted in a general strike in 1934, employers in that city never even called on the onetime King of the Strikebreakers.[194] In June of that year his army failed to turn the tide for the Milwaukee Electric Railway and Light Company. The majority of the community, including Mayor Daniel C. Hoan, who ordered the arrest of 150 of Bergoff's men,

Fig. 2.11   When elevator operators threatened to strike in the fall of 1934, veteran strikebreakers jammed into Bergoff's office looking for "work." Photograph for *Fortune* by Aitkins ©1935 Time, Inc. All rights reserved.

sympathized with the strikers. Those who escaped the mayor's roundup found themselves outnumbered by an enraged populace and escorted to the railroad station.[195] During the textile strikes later that summer, when executives at the Bibb Manufacturing Company of Porterdale, Georgia, called on the Bergoff brothers' services, they watched his army flee before local officials.[196] In spite of his conviction that "there'll be more strikes in 1935 than ever in history, and it don't make me mad," the next year brought him only a lengthy court battle and more disappointments. Charging that he withheld pay from the men he dispatched to Porterdale, the Industrial Commissioner for the state of New York, Elmer F. Andrews, recommended that the secretary of state "hold a hearing for the purpose of determining whether the license of the Bergoff Detective Service Inc. should be revoked."[197] Compounding his woes, the New York State Department of Labor added charges that he not only misled workers about the nature of the job in Porterdale, but also violated workmen's compensation laws by having these men sign waivers protecting the agency from any claims. Although he put up a vigorous defense, telling the court, "In the history of my campaigns I've never cheated a man out of a penny," the decision of the court went against him. He, however, believed "there's still plenty of demand for my services."[198] His prediction proved more than just bravado.

Even as his name was dragged before the public, employers continued to call upon the agency he headed. In the summer of 1936, for example, the Bergoff brothers found themselves playing an important role in an ingenious anti-union campaign drafted by James H. Rand Jr. Hailed by the National Association of Manufacturers as the modern answer to labor unrest, his "Mohawk Valley Formula" utilized Bergoff's men in a traditional way but also included a couple of creative variations. Although he earned a substantial reward for his efforts during this campaign, this strike marked the beginning of the end for the King of the Strikebreakers.

Less than two weeks after workers at seven Remington Rand plants walked away from their posts, one hundred of Bergoff's men appeared in a field across from his plant in Tonawanda, New York, and began marching toward its gates. Their instructions, Bergoff later claimed, "were to try to peacefully go into the plant as though they were looking for work."[199] The incident Bergoff and Rand planned on was not long in coming as "two hundred strikers awaited them." When they met, "the two groups engaged in combat. Bricks and stones were hurled and punches were thrown."[200] Rand staged this march knowing that the strikebreakers' "presence would infuriate the strikers to the point of combat," members of the NLRB concluded.[201] He expected violence, for he arranged for an underling to take moving pictures of the melee. Bergoff, who believed that a record of the confrontation "was good stuff for getting an injunction," proved an astute observer, for in addition to publishing many of the pictures in local papers, Rand used this material as evidence to obtain a temporary injunction against the strikers.[202] In another instance in late June, at the same time a "for sale" sign appeared outside the Remmington Rand plant in Middletown, Connecticut, company officials began advertising for millwrights to assist in "dismantling machinery and skidding machinery for shipment."[203] Rand never planned to hire those who applied, however, for Bergoff had already agreed to supply him with fifty-nine "millwrights." Although they carried millwright cards, they knew little about tearing down a plant. Bergoff later testified to this fact when he told the NLRB: "A man, a fink, as you call him in the newspapers, he is anything; he may be a carpenter today, a plumber tomorrow, a bricklayer the next day; this particular day they were millwrights."[204] That they looked as if they were ready to move this operation was what was important. When Rand announced that he had decided not to relocate his facility and, with only limited positions to be filled, would soon reopen, the strikers quickly returned to their posts.[205] When it was all over, Rand congratulated Bergoff, saying, "Now you have done wonderful work."[206] He paid the Bergoff Service Bureau and seven other detective agencies $145,000 for the two months the strike dragged on.[207]

While Rand may have been pleased with the Red Demon's efforts, shortly after his workers returned to their posts the United States District Court for the District of Connecticut indicted both men for transporting strikebreakers across state lines.[208] Although federal commissions periodically condemned professional strikebreaking, for years Congress remained immune to their request to legislate against this sordid industry. National lawmakers finally acted with the introduction of a bill by Senator James F. Byrnes of South Carolina in August 1935. According to a Senate report, the need for such legislation resulted from the "development of organizations styled 'detective agencies,' employing thousands of

men who are sent into various States of the Union where labor controversies exist, . . . to have such persons interfere with citizens . . . engaged
in lawful activities."[209] The introduction of such forces, members of the
House believed, "fans the fires of resentment, and incites further strife
and bloodshed."[210] On June 24, 1936, the day before Bergoff shipped
his men to Rand's plant in Middletown, President Roosevelt signed
the Byrnes Act into law, making it a felony to transport persons in interstate commerce with the intent to employ them to obstruct the rights
of peaceful picketing.[211] Although Judge Carroll D. Hincks acquitted
Bergoff and his client, the Red Demon was coming to realize that his
tactics of intimidation and confrontation were becoming passé. Nearly
three decades after opening his detective agency, he closed his office and
retired in 1936.[212]

As the federal government became increasingly involved in regulating the relations between workers and employers as the nation moved
further into the twentieth century, those unique American economic
axioms that protected strikebreakers and those they served became out-
dated. New Deal labor legislation ushered in a new economic environment in which the government provided labor a degree of protection
by institutionalizing their relationship with the business community.
Moreover, although a handful of professional strikebreakers found ways
around federal regulatory legislation, restricted not only by the Byrnes
Act but by a public that had come to look askance at the utilization of
thugs, many employers now rejected such blatant tactics. Ironically
enough, as employers increasingly came to favor more subtle anti-union
methods, the longtime King of the Strikebreakers came to enjoy a degree
of the prominence he had longed for. While the national press sent
reporters to interview him, a London-based newspaper inquired into his
views on industrial relations via a trans-Atlantic telephone.[213]

3

SPIES, PROPAGANDISTS, MISSIONARIES, AND HOOKERS

The Era of Industrial Espionage

THE SAME YEAR ONETIME King of the Strikebreakers Pearl Bergoff retired, Robert Pinkerton announced that his firm would no longer "furnish its employes [*sic*] to any client for the exclusive purpose of providing workmen to take the place of a client's striking employees, nor to physically protect employes [*sic*] . . . while a labor strike is in progress."[1] Like Bergoff, the Pinkertons had come to realize that the days when strikebreaking generals marshaled thousands of finks to take the place of strikers had come to an end. Rather than turn its back on a lucrative market, the Pinkerton Agency, as well as many similar firms, "preferred to place emphasis on its undercover work which being secret, created less antagonism."[2] Though it was nothing new, as laissez-faire capitalism came under attack after the twentieth century dawned spying on workers came to play a larger role in the business community's offensive against labor. By the mid- to late 1930s, as a new social and political environment further challenged the employer's right to do as he pleased and restrictive legislation prohibited other unionbusting strategies, espionage took on a new importance. By that decade more than two hundred agencies, including the Pinkerton National Detective Agency, the most important supplier of industrial spies in the country, offered its clients undercover operatives.[3]

Under the direction of Allan Pinkerton, the Pinkerton National Detective Agency, the first agency to begin offering employers labor discipline services, began providing "spotters" to expose dishonest and lazy railroad conductors as early as 1855.[4] Railroads, Pinkerton argued, lost between 40 and 60 percent of their profits from conductor dishonesty.[5] With the rapid growth of the transportation network following the Civil War, he established testing programs in a number of railroad hubs, including New York, Chicago, and Philadelphia.[6] Pinkerton's spotter program eventually unraveled. Following a train accident in November 1872, papers found on the body of one of its operatives revealed the agency's deceitful practices, generating public anger as well as national curiosity.[7] By the end of that year, the man who came to head the Pinkerton Agency, Robert Pinkerton, ended this service, concluding that, in the eyes of the business community, individual acts of dishonesty paled in comparison to the growing threat of collective conspiratorial violence.[8]

The following year Pinkerton operative James McParlan infiltrated the secret society of Irish-American coal miners known as the Molly Maguires; by gathering enough information to hang ten "Mollies," he

Fig. 3.1 The founder of Pinkerton National Detective Agency, Allan Pinkerton was the first in a long line of entrepreneurs to recognize the opportunities inherent in the increasingly violent capital-labor relationship. Library of Congress, Prints and Photographs Division, LC-USZ 62-117576.

sent the agency off in this new direction. As strikes and lockouts came to dominate industrial relations during the next two decades, "industrial work" came to play a more important role for the agency.[9] During this period of industrial unrest the Pinkertons skillfully played upon the business community's growing fear. "At this time when there is so much dissatisfaction among the laboring classes . . . would [it] not be well for employers . . . to keep a close watch for designing men among their own employees?" they asked in a circular in 1889.[10] This appeal proved effective, as the agency established fifteen new offices between 1890 and 1910.[11]

Helping their clients to break a number of strikes—including two of the most bitterly contested labor struggles of the period, the Coeur d'Alene mining strike of 1892 and the Chicago, Burlington, and Quincy Railroad strike four years earlier—Pinkerton undercover operatives proved themselves a formidable anti-union weapon.[12] In the wake of this latter dispute, railroad unionists so feared Pinkerton spies that during a convention of the Brotherhood of Locomotive Engineers held in Richmond, Virginia, in the fall of 1888, all meetings were held behind closed doors. Delegates also organized a special committee to search out hiding places spies might utilize. Their efforts failed, for two Pinkerton operatives attended the convention and recorded all the minutes of the meeting.[13]

Along with the operatives who infiltrated the locomotive engineers' meeting, this agency employed a number of undercover men skilled at destroying unions from within, including its most celebrated agent, Charles A. Siringo. Working out of the Denver office he played a significant role in bringing the Coeur d'Alene strike to an end. Employed by

Fig. 3.2 Pinkerton National Detective Agency letterhead with its famous open eye and motto "We Never Sleep," ca. 1900. Morris B. Schnapper Collection, George Meany Memorial Archives, AFL/CIO, Silver Spring, Maryland.

the Mine Owners' Protective Association (MOA), he hired on at the Gem mine, in Gem, Idaho, in the waning days of the summer of 1891.[14] Under the name C. Leon Allison, he joined the local union and, by buying drinks and lending money to his fellow miners, won a place among its membership. By December of that year, they elected him to the post of secretary, which he bragged "was a useful position . . . since it would give me access to all the [union] books and records."[15]

Reporting all union matters to his employers, Siringo enabled the mine owners to outmaneuver the miners on a number of occasions.[16] When strikers planned to waylay a train of incoming strikebreakers, for example, he warned the mine owners, who dropped off their replacement workers where they were not expected.[17] In another instance, when the president of the miners' union, Oliver Hughes, ordered him to remove a page from the union record book containing evidence that strikers considered flooding the mines, he ripped it out and mailed it to the association.[18] Siringo also told his employer's clients what they wanted to hear. In one report he claimed that George A. Pettibone and other union officials were "dangerous anarchists, who had completely duped the hard-working miners and were formulating demands" to which mine officials could never agree.[19]

Although he went to great lengths to keep his identity secret—including mailing his reports to an address in St. Paul, Minnesota, where the Pinkerton Agency maintained a secret office—when the MOA's newspaper, the *Coeur d'Alene Barbarian,* began publishing union secrets, suspicion fell on him.[20] He had had access to classified information as union secretary, and strikers wanted to know why a page was missing from the record book that had been in his charge. He argued that President Hughes had ordered him to remove the page that detailed their plans to flood the mines. Now, "shunned by many union members," he quit the union but stayed on in the employ of the MOA.[21]

As the lockout stretched into its sixth month, the strikers' frustration began to build as strikebreakers poured into the mining district. More important, most believed that their onetime recording secretary had sold them out. Although union leaders urged the rank and file to eschew violence, on July 11 they erupted in anger, blowing up the Frisco mine in Gem and capturing the Gem mine and 150 nonunion miners and company guards. Within minutes of the explosion, hundreds of strikers converged on Siringo's boardinghouse. His escape only inflamed them further. Dropping down through a hole he sawed in the floor, he crawled half a block under the raised wooden sidewalk. "It was a nerve-tying business . . . I could look up and actually see the men and hear what they were saying. If one of them happened to glance down and spot me, my life would not be worth a second's purchase," he later wrote.[22] While the miners searched for him, he fled to the hills above Coeur d'Alene.

Although the miners considered the battle over and issued a statement deploring "the unfortunate affair at Gem and Frisco," violence provided the mine owners with the excuse they needed to demand state intervention.[23] Three days after the battle at the Gem mine, Governor Norman H. Willey declared martial law in the Coeur d'Alene region and ordered in six companies of the Idaho National Guard to suppress "insurrection and violence."[24] Assured of protection, on July 14 Siringo came down out of the mountains to identify fourteen union leaders and participants in the attack upon the Gem and Frisco mines. For days he was busy "putting unruly cattle in the bull pen," he wrote.[25] Providing eyewitness testimony, he helped convict four of the fourteen union leaders at trials in Coeur d'Alene and Boise in August.[26] By the late fall of 1892, after a year and a half on the job, Siringo closed his operation in Idaho and returned to Denver. The following year angry miners formed the Western Federation of Miners (WFM) and insisted that employment of "any Pinkerton detectives" be outlawed.[27] Their request went unheeded as undercover men became an even more important anti-union tool.

By the dawn of the age of muckraking and reform, it became clear that more employers were turning to espionage services, like those supplied by E. H. Murphy, who once told a midwestern industrialist: "We have the reputation of being several jumps ahead of the old way of settling capital and labor difficulties. . . . Our service aims to keep our clients informed through the medium of intelligence reports."[28] As early as 1904, Samuel Gompers concluded that progressive liberal public opinion was prompting employers to become more clandestine in their anti-union activities.[29] A few years later delegates to the Massachusetts state AFL convention concluded that private detective agencies had not only "assumed formidable proportions" but threatened to Russianize American society.[30] In this age of progressive reform, executives, most of whom were comfortable, elderly, and had never dealt with an aggressive organized workforce before, were inclined to put their trust in those like Captain B. Kelcher of the C.B.K. Detective Bureau of New York, who informed one prospective client that his firm did "not handle strike work" but rather "prevent[ed] strikes."[31]

The burgeoning number of trade union journal editorials devoted to the evils of espionage also provides evidence of the growing importance of industrial spying as well as labor's increasing frustration in the face of this anti-union weapon.[32] Editors for the *Brotherhood of Locomotive Firemen's Magazine* epitomized the feelings of most unionists in their headline of June 1906: "A Long Established Fundamental and Vital Principal [collective bargaining] Superseded by 'Secret Service' Methods."[33] Three years later they hinted that death would be too good for the labor spy.[34] "Big" Bill Haywood voiced his hatred for labor spies when on a postcard mass-produced for dissemination he wrote: "That you may know how small a detective is, you can take a hair and punch the pith out of it and in the hollow hair you can put the hearts and souls of 40,000 detectives and they will still rattle."[35] Organized labor's growing animosity resulted not only from the spies' insidious nature but also because of their increasing numbers and their ability to destroy unions.

Little wonder Haywood held the labor spy in contempt. Under direction of James McParlan, the Denver office of the Pinkerton Agency controlled a number of operatives within the WFM, including A. W. Gratias. In 1903, when mine operators found themselves involved in a struggle with the union they regarded as dangerously un-American, they turned to this agency. In Colorado City, as soon as miners left the mines, union relief administrator Gratias, or, as he was known to managers, No. 42, pared down relief expenditures "so as to cause dissatisfaction and get the men against the union."[36] The next year, members of his local elected him president and sent him to a WFM annual convention, from where he supplied his employers with voluminous reports on union activities.[37] Pinkerton operative No. 42 was not alone, for secretary of the Mill and Smeltermen's Union local 125 of the WFM was Pinkerton operative No. 5, A. H. Crane. In charge of his union's books, he supplied his employer's client with a complete list of union sympathizers as well as copies of correspondence between that local and WFM headquarters. After managers let go a number of union men, union officials finally caught him when it was remembered that he was seen making a number of unexplained telephone calls.[38]

Although it dominated much of the unionbusting industry, the Pinkerton Agency was not without competition. By the twentieth century, besieged industrialists could find, in the telephone directory of any large city, a host of labor-spy services listed under such euphemisms as "industrial engineers," "private detectives," and "labor conciliators."[39] Other such agencies advertised their services in business journals. "We are prepared," one agency informed potential customers in the May 1905 issue of *American Industries,* "to place secret operatives who are skilled mechanics in any shop, mill or factory, to discover whether any [labor] organizing is being done."[40] In another example, in 1906 officers of the Corporations Auxiliary Company announced to prospective clients that they would have "several delegates" at the twenty-sixth annual convention of the American Federation of Labor. "For the sum of fifteen dollars" they offered to provide customers "with a full and complete report of the entire proceedings."[41] Some agencies went so far as to send secret

Fig. 3.3 A. H. Crane, an officer in a local of the Western Federation of Miners, also served as Pinkerton operative #5. In addition to supplying his employers with detailed reports on union activities, he devastated this local by prompting a premature strike. From Morris Friedman, *The Pinkerton Labor Spy* (New York: Wilshire Books, 1907).

operatives into a prospective client's factory without permission. They would then submit to the startled manager a report of their investigation, revealing a conspiracy complete with tales of sabotage and brewing strikes. For example, in 1920, a solicitor for the Marshall Service warned the Kansas Flour Mills Company that not only were their workers organized but 60 percent of the men were associated with the IWW.[42]

By the time of the steel strike of 1919, spying on workers became such an accepted business practice that steel company executives freely handed over to Interworld Church Movement investigators six hundred spy reports. Compiled by the Sherman Service Company and the Corporations Auxiliary Company, these accounts ranged from the "illiterate scribblings of professional parasites to the most accurate transcriptions of union locals' secret meetings."[43] The latter agency encouraged its operatives to "try at all times to find out who is a member of a labor organization." To this end, these men were to "mingle with the fellows in the noon hour, in the factory and on the streetcar."[44] Carefully instructed on how to play the role of the trade unionist to ensure anonymity, "spies in this organization [IWW] were ordered to dress in old overalls and old shoes and not to shave. Spies in these various communist parties were allowed to dress somewhat better. Operatives specializing on the socialist party were advised to dress like middle class folks and those working in the A. F. of L. unions to adopt the customs and dress of the craft to which they were assigned."[45] Far from simply reporting upon union activities, by borrowing ideas "from modern employment managers, from civic federations; from the spokesman of the open shop," all of which emphasized "getting on and thrift and self made success," spies in the employ of this agency encouraged workers to reject unionization and return to their jobs.[46] "I trust . . . I shall be able to influence a good many men to return to work," one agent, Z-16, boasted to his employers during this strike.[47]

Little more than a decade later, as the economic environment became increasingly more progressive and, as worried business people came to feel under attack from all sides, espionage came "to be a common, almost universal, practice in American industry." Recognizing the liabilities inherent in overt forms of labor discipline services, a virtual "blue book of American industry," including thirty-two mining companies, twenty-eight firms associated with the automotive industry, and an equal number

THE
WILLIAM J. BURNS
INTERNATIONAL DETECTIVE AGENCY, INC.

TELEPHONE: BARCLAY 7600   CABLE ADDRESS: WILBURNS

ATLANTA	CLEVELAND	HOUSTON	MONTREAL	PITTSBURGH	ST. LOUIS
BALTIMORE	DALLAS	KANSAS CITY	NEW ORLEANS	PORTLAND	SEATTLE
BOSTON	DENVER	LONDON	NEW YORK	RICHMOND	SPOKANE
BUFFALO	DES MOINES	LOS ANGELES	OKLAHOMA CITY	SAN FRANCISCO	TORONTO
CHICAGO	DETROIT	MEMPHIS	PARIS	SALT LAKE CITY	VANCOUVER
CINCINNATI	EL PASO	MINNEAPOLIS	PHILADELPHIA	SAN ANTONIO	WASHINGTON, D. C.

ADDRESS ALL REMITTANCES AND COMMUNICATIONS DIRECT TO AGENCY

WOOLWORTH BUILDING
NEW YORK

To the American Manufacturer:

An era of prosperity is apparent; likewise an era of competition. To the Manufacturer who elects to enter the race for supremacy in supplying the world's markets with goods, the carrying over of last year's unsolved problem may prove a serious handicap. Why carry that excess burden of perplexing problems into the new year to clog up your machinery; increase costs and create an atmosphere of uncertainty?

Perhaps this thought was suggested at your Board of Directors' Meeting immediately following the stock taking period. In the anticipation of greater business you have doubtless instructed your engineering staff to make ready the necessary plant equipment, but the Manufacturers' preparations are not complete until the human engineering problem is solved. The Industrial Specialist to-day is a recognized factor where economic policies are pursued, and in no case does he become more essential to the Manufacturer than when his skill is directed to the human side of industry.

The Industrial Service supplied by the William J. Burns International Detective Agency, Inc., has become an asset to Modern Industrial Enterprise and a Burns Industrial Specialist quietly working in your plant has not only the training and intelligence to give you a most intimate acquaintance with your employes, but to reveal also in a comprehensive daily report any other factor tending to impede the daily progress toward the desired goal.

If you have bid strong for 1922 business let us determine for you the loyal, or disloyal status of your organization during the first quarter of the year, rather than the last.

The questions suggested to Manufacturers during the first month of each year are invariably these:

Through what channels have profits leaked away during the past year?
What percentage could be charged to thefts?
To Disloyal Propaganda instituted by the Professional Agitator?
To Carelessness and Indifference?
To Collusion between Employes and Outside Criminals?
To Plant Secrets divulged by employes?
To Strife and Jealousies between Departments?
To Incompetent and Arrogant Foremen?
To Barriers before Individual Effort and Enthusiasm?
To Salesmen's Lethargy?
Are they concerned about the Overhead?
Do their Reports reflect the true buying Market?
Is the Pay Roll safe and are its Carriers unduly exposed?
Our Service is designed to deal efficiently with these subjects and dispel the doubt that prompts the query.

An inquiry on your letterhead or a telephone call to any one of our offices indicated above, will bring a representative to your office, incurring no obligation on your part.

Raymond J Burns

Fig. 3.4 Advertising in a trade publication in the early 1920s, the Burns Detective Agency emphasized its ability to uncover not only dishonest employees, but also "professional agitators," a euphemism for labor organizers. From *American Industries* (February 1922).

Contract #251

TELEGRAM
923-924
NEW YORK LIFE
BUILDING

TELEPHONE
BELL MAIN 5005

THE MARSHALL SERVICE
OF KANSAS;

P. O. BOX 1058

BE IT KNOWN TO ALL CONCERNED that the MARSHALL SERVICE, of Kansas City, Kansas, hereinafter known as the party of the first part, and _____ of _____, hereinafter known as the party of the second part, CONTRACT AND AGREE as follows.

FIRST: The party of the first part shall, without cost to the party of the second part, maintain and support a necessary number of trained and experienced Operatives, in such various parts of the country as may be necessary to perform the following services, for the party of the second part:

    A. Obtain information regarding any actual, or threatened labor troubles, or agitation, which may directly effect the interests of the party of the second part.

    B. Obtain information concerning labor troubles and agitation existing in various parts of the country, which may not directly concern the party of the second part, but which may be of benefit to the party of the second part, as useful information.

    C. To obtain information regarding any act, or acts, of any person, or persons, or organization, or corporation, which may, or might, have the affect of disrupting the efficiency organization of the employees, or the working organization, of the party of the second part.

SECOND: The party of the first part shall maintain and support an effective working organization of trained and experienced Operatives, who shall be experienced Flour Mill Workers, and one or more of these Operatives shall be, upon request of the party of the second part, assigned to the Mill of the party of the second part, and shall remain in the service of that Mill as long as it may be necessary, and shall endeavor to protect the said Mill against:

    A. Robbery, Theft or Arson.
    B. Labor Troubles and Agitation.
    C. Strikes or Mob Violence.
    D. Any illegal act, punishable under the Criminal Law.

THIRD: The party of the second part shall remunerate the party of the first part, with a yearly payment, which shall become due at the signing of this Contract, proportioned to the various mills as follows:

Daily Capacity	Per year	Daily Capacity	Per year
Mills from 100 to 500 bbls.	$ 25.00	Mills from 5100 to 6000 bbls.	$350.00
" " 600 to 1000 "	50.00	" " 6100 to 7000 "	400.00
" " 1100 to 2000 "	100.00	" " 7100 to 8000 "	450.00
" " 2100 to 3000 "	150.00	" " 8100 to 9000 "	500.00
" " 3100 to 4000 "	200.00	" " 9100 to 20000 "	550.00
" " 4100 to 5000 "	250.00	" " 21000 to 40000 "	600.00

FOURTH: The party of the second part shall be entitled to receive, without cost, any information or advice that the party of the first part is competent to extend, and the party of the first part shall receive remuneration at the rate of $9 per day and all expenses, for each and every Operative, assigned to the service of the party of the second part upon request, from the time said Operative leaves Kansas City until return—less any and all wages which may be paid said Operative for his work as an employee in the Mill or service of the party of the second part.

IN WITNESS WHEREOF THIS CONTRACT AND AGREEMENT, which shall remain in full force and effect for a period of One Year from date, has been signed in ORIGINAL and DUPLICATE by both parties hereunto on this ___ day of _____, 1920.

PARTY OF THE FIRST PART.   THE MARSHALL SERVICE.

By _____

PARTY OF THE SECOND PART _____

By _____

Fig. 3.5 The Marshall Service contracted to provide a Minneapolis-based miller's association with operatives skilled in thwarting "Strikes or Mob Violence," as well as in uncovering "Labor Troubles and Agitation." Members of the association paid for this service based on their mills' outputs. From J. E. Spielman, *The Stool Pigeon and the Open Shop Movement* (Minneapolis: The American Publishing Co., 1923).

of food processing concerns, relied upon labor spies by the middle of the Depression decade.[48] Testifying before a Senate hearing on anti-union practices, one member of the NLRB estimated that American industrialists spent over eighty million dollars a year spying on their workers.[49]

One major company, General Motors, for example, invested $994,000 for undercover work during a two-year period surrounding the Congress of Industrial Organizations' (CIO) drive to unionize the auto industry.[50] In addition to its largest anti-union contractor, the Pinkerton Agency, this automaker employed thirteen spy agencies, including the Railway

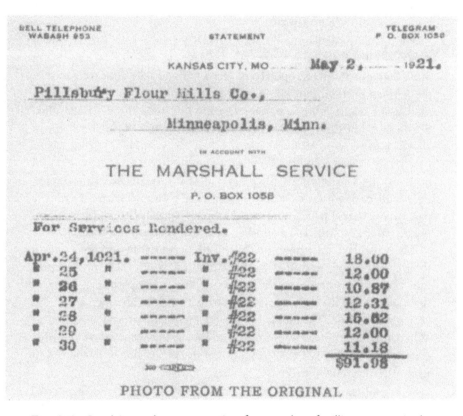

Fig. 3.6 Supplying undercover operatives for a number of milling concerns in the upper Midwest, the Marshall Service billed Pillsbury Flour Mills more than ninety dollars during April of 1922 for the disruptive machinations of one agent. From J. E. Spielman, *The Stool Pigeon and the Open Shop Movement* (Minneapolis: The American Publishing Co., 1923).

Audit and Inspection Company, the William J. Burns Company, and the Corporations Auxiliary Company.[51] GM's dependence upon espionage services reached its final addictive stages when the company utilized Pinkerton spies to spy upon operatives in the employ of other agencies within its plants.[52] In addition to General Motors, the Pinkerton Agency provided spy service for three hundred other firms during the 1930s.[53] The year before the auto strike, it operated out of twenty-seven offices and grossed over two million dollars.[54] Between 1933 and 1935 it employed more than twelve hundred undercover operatives.[55] The Pinkerton National Detective Agency had not only plenty of business but also a host of competitors.

For its many clients, the Pinkerton Agency (and similar firms) proved a valuable ally during this strike-laden decade. In addition to employing more than one thousand operatives, it maintained sixty-four spies within the railroad brotherhoods. Seventeen of its agents held union cards with the United Textile Workers of America, and the ranks of the International Brotherhood of Electrical Workers contained twenty Pinkerton men. In all, the agency wormed its way into ninety-three unions.[56] Other agencies were also well established behind union lines. By 1935, the Cleveland office of the Corporations Auxiliary Company controlled thirty spies, twenty-three of whom were union members.[57] "In my experience for the past twenty years I have found out that there is stools [sic] in every union organization," an official of another detective agency once boasted.[58]

On a regular basis these men submitted reports on activities within their clients' plants and their workers' union halls. In their most important function, ascertaining the names of union sympathizers, some of these men, like Pinkerton operative Fred Weber, who obtained a position as a night janitor in a union office in Cincinnati, proved ingenious.[59] When a strike erupted, spies in the employ of one agency were not only expected "to go out with the boys, go on the picket line with them" but were also to phone in every two or three hours.[60]

While operatives directly in the employ of these agencies generated most undercover reports, some were written by workers who had been duped, or, in the spy's parlance, "hooked," into this sordid profession. Roped in gradually, they first reported on innocuous offenses, such as malingering, and then on the thoughts and opinions of their coworkers.[61] "Hookers," or those who enlisted such men, often preyed upon those with a grudge against the union or those in need. "Red" Kulh, a veteran hooker, told a Senate committee: "Well first you look your prospect over ... if he is married that is preferable." Once a man was singled out, he went on to testify, "You go after him with this extra money." Often led to believe that they worked for an insurance agency or interested stockholders, many never suspected that their employers received the reports they drafted.[62] Those willing to sell out their colleagues earned from twenty-five to seventy-five dollars a month, a welcome additional income for many during hard times. During the first half of 1936, the Pinkerton Agency paid out $240,000 to such men.[63] While many freed themselves once they understood whom they worked for, others—like John Davidson, who wrote in his report to the Railway Audit and Inspection Company in 1935, "I have known Ferguson for twenty years and Kepler for ten and now I am selling them out as they tell me most everything"—proved effective anti-union tools.[64] While no evidence of such activity can be found prior to the 1930s, by that decade nearly every espionage agency, including the National Corporation Service, which estimated that 70 percent of their operatives had been recruited in this fashion, utilized their clients' employees to report on their fellow workers.[65]

With the help of this fifth column, anti-union employers quietly ended their labor problems by discharging those who were less than loyal. In early 1935, for example, the Fruehauf Trailer Company of Detroit, Michigan, fired nine workers and threatened to let go three others for involvement in union activities after the treasurer of one local, a Pinkerton operative, turned union rosters and dues ledgers over to management. Chairman of the National Labor Relations Board (NLRB) J. Warren Madden reported in regard to this case: "The mystery and deadly certainty with which this scheme [espionage] operated was so baffling to the men that they each suspected the others, were afraid to meet or to talk and the union was completely broken."[66] Further evidence of the fear Pinkerton spies inspired can be found in a report filed the following year by L. L. Letteer Jr. Working undercover in a General Motors plant in Atlanta during the United Auto Workers' (UAW) drive to unionize the auto industry, he reported: "Those labor unions were so hot, crying about spies, that everything was at fever pitch and they look at each other with blood in their eyes."[67]

Not only well ensconced within union ranks, many undercover operatives occupied leadership roles. Nearly one-third of those in the employ of the Pinkerton Agency, for instance, held high positions, including one national vice-presidency, fourteen local presidencies, eight local vice-presidencies, and numerous secretaryships.[68] They also controlled forty-three operatives within company unions, among them one president, three recording secretaries, and one chairman.[69] From such lofty positions these men created factions and disagreements. For example, after election to a high position within a local of the International Association of Machinists, Sam Brady, a veteran Pinkerton operative, damaged this union by inciting a premature strike.[70] Earlier, he boasted to his supervisors, "This is an easy one to handle as there are about only two men in it that are really interested in the organization work and they are easily discouraged."[71] In another example, once the CIO began its drive to unionize the auto industry, Pinkerton operatives drove out all but five officers from a local of the United Auto Workers (UAW) in Lansing, Michigan. The remaining five worked for the Pinkerton brothers.[72] Other agencies proved equally destructive, including the Burns Agency, which "effectually crushed" unionization efforts at the Montgomery Ward Company of Portland, Oregon, in 1938, or the International Auxiliary Company, which so wrecked a union at the Underwood Elliot Fisher Company plant that its membership dropped from more than twenty-five hundred to fewer than seventy-five.[73] Still, if such schemes proved less than successful, most agencies' bags of dirty tricks included a host of other machinations.

In addition to supplying undercover operatives and agent provocateurs to those employers frightened by the specter of a unionized workforce, many anti-union contractors conducted whispering campaigns for their clients. Such propaganda had been a part of these agencies' arsenals at least as early as World War I. By the Depression decade, members of the NLRB believed propaganda disseminated by missionaries—undercover operatives who created dissension on the picket line and in the union halls and engendered public opposition to strikes by planting rumors—proved "the most common form of interference with self-organization engaged in by employers."[74] Among the dozens of letters of solicitation Republic Steel Corporation received before the Little Steel strike, at least three detective agencies offered missionary services.[75] An executive of one agency, W. Howard Downey and Associates, wrote: "We have a whole kit of expressions . . . that have proved themselves in the handling of industrial disturbances time and again. After hearing a few remarks that we have up our sleeves you should see how apprehensive a striker becomes."[76] Not only a common form of labor control, members of the NLRB believed that the "pressure exerted on workers" by missionaries often proved "overwhelming."[77] Indeed, in 1935 McGuffin Agency operatives ended a strike among member firms of the Youngstown Automobile Dealers' Association in about "three weeks" and during the Hazel-Atlas Glass Company strike the previous year "put out propaganda so fast . . . the union was practically stopped in its tracks despite the head start it had" and within a short while "was pretty well washed up," one agent reported.[78]

Recognizing that strikes often hung precariously on the support of the workers' spouses as well as local merchants, who occasionally extended credit to union members, missionaries often directed their whispering campaigns toward the strikers' families and community. According to one undercover agent, during a strike directed against the Stevens Metal Products Company, female operatives in the employ of the McGuffin Detective Agency got some supplies of face cream or furniture polish or something they would give away and pretend to be demonstrators, so as to get into the houses of the workers in the plant and stay there long enough to put out their propaganda while demonstrating. They would bring the conversation around to the union, and one of their favorite gags was to tell how their husbands or brothers or fathers joined a union a year or two previously in some other town and was pulled off his good job by the union and had never been able to get a job since, and they had to take on demonstrating work in order to support their family.[79] Other operatives met with local merchants who were shown "how big a payroll [sic] loss would result if the union wasn't stopped, . . . and got them to talk against the union among the customers." The strike was ended, he boasted, in less than three weeks.[80]

With a Democratic Congress and president fostering a new relationship between employers and their workers, by the 1930s anti-union practitioners developed a number of new ruses to meet the needs of their clients. For example, after the enactment of the National Industrial Recovery Act (NIRA) in 1933, rather than bargain collectively with outside unions—as this legislation encouraged—employers began setting up less threatening company unions with the assistance of espionage agencies. Many unions of this genre "which sometimes appear[ed] to spring up spontaneously in industrial communities to forestall union drives [were] . . . frequently inspired and directed by labor spies," members of the La Follette committee believed.[81] The Pinkerton Agency became heavily involved in this activity, controlling forty-three operatives within company unions.[82] To convince workers to join such an organization, experienced operatives "would talk and talk against the union," using arguments such as "Why pay dues to a lot of organizers, presidents, secretaries, one thing or another . . . now if we keep a company union we don't pay any dues," one agent testified.[83] The Butler Service of New York, whose officers boasted of forming "hundreds of such organizations," the Railway Audit and Inspection Company, which played a role "in starting a lot of employees' associations," and the McGuffin Agency offered similar services.[84] For employees, such as those at the Taylor-Winfield Company plant in Warren, Ohio, such tactics proved deadly as this latter agency helped to destroy an outside union while establishing a company union at their firm in less than four months.[85]

By the mid 1930s, as the public's frustration with organized labor began to mount in the wake of increasing strike violence "it . . . [was] not unusual for private detectives and citizens' committees to work hand in hand" to establish anti-union citizens' groups to help their clients marshal this anger.[86] While little evidence of this sort of ruse can be found prior to the 1930s, by the middle of the Depression decade, a number of espionage agencies became involved in establishing such organizations. Shortly after the CIO began its drive to organize the Little Steel companies in 1936, for example, a solicitor for a New York agency told Tom Girdler of Republic Steel that "the foremost and most important work in cases where a strike impends" was "to organize the inert mass of citizens . . . under the direction of . . . trained propagandists-organizers so that a handful of professional union organizers cannot [sic] force the community to dance to their terroristic music."[87] While Girdler failed to avail his company of such services, other executives, according to members of the NLRB, found these committees "particularly effective in breaking . . . union[s]." For example, with the help of the A. A. Anher Agency— which, among other strategies, established a "citizens' committee"—the

Brown Shoe Company quickly ended a unionization drive by the Boot and Shoe Workers Union that same year.[88]

After better than a half century of disciplining their clients' workforce, the Pinkerton Agency, the A. A. Anher Agency, and their many competitors fell victim to their own successes and the exposure of their activities before a Democratic Congress anxious to uphold labor's right to bargain collectively. Although the public had demonstrated only a limited interest in reining in anti-union practitioners over the previous half century, by the Depression decade a new social climate enabled Congress to launch a thorough investigation into their activities. For the first time in the course of American history, not only had an administration made the welfare of the industrial worker a primary concern, but the reverence shown for business and private property came to an abrupt halt with the changed attitudes brought about by the worst modern depression. Moreover, in 1935, the American Federation of Labor, supported by the American Civil Liberties Union and much of the American clergy, called for an "immediate and thorough" inquiry into anti-union activities.[89] While such efforts may have generated public support for an inquiry, it was the frustration experienced by the NLRB in implementing the guidelines of the Wagner Act that finally prompted congressional action.

By the end of 1935, both the Wagner Act and the board this legislation created were in serious trouble as the business community not only refused to comply with its provisions but also continued utilizing specialists to cow workers into submission. Believing that only a public outcry would force them to honor organized labor's right to bargain collectively, Heber Blankenhorn, an NLRB staff member and a former investigator for the Interchurch Inquiry turned to a young senator from Wisconsin, Robert M. La Follette Jr., hoping he would initiate an inquiry into those anti-union practices that plagued organized labor.[90] Although he initially demonstrated little interest, in late March of 1936 La Follette introduced to Congress Senate Resolution 266, directing the Committee on Education and Labor to begin an investigation into violations of workers' civil liberties.[91]

When preliminary hearings on this resolution began in early April 1936, the first witness, chairman of the National Labor Relations Board, J. Warren Madden, set the tone of this inquiry when he testified that the "very dirty business of espionage was . . . the chief obstacle to the realization" of government-backed collective bargaining.[92] With the aid of the American Civil Liberties Union and the behind-the-scenes efforts of Blankenhorn, Senate Resolution 266 moved slowly but steadily through the 74th Congress, finally to be approved on June 6, 1936.[93] According to Blankenhorn, the primary objective of the committee hearings, which began in late September of that year, was "to really dig out the rats and those responsible for them."[94]

Although members of what came to be known as the La Follette committee looked into numerous aspects of the employer-labor relationship, labor discipline services provided by espionage and other anti-union agencies occupied the majority of their attention. After distributing more than eight hundred questionnaires to such agencies, the committee called to the nation's capital officials of five of the largest firms: Railway Audit and Inspection Company, Pinkerton National Detective Agency, Corporations Auxiliary Company, National Corporation Service, and the William J. Burns International Detective Agency. Along with victimized workers and union officials, a handful of industrial captains also appeared. The senators not only required the latter group to turn over all documents relating to the use of anti-union agencies from January 1, 1933, until the time of the hearings, they also impounded the records of their mercenaries.[95] From both they encountered duplicity, evasion, and open defiance. Railway Audit and Inspection Company officials refused to testify or hand over corporate records. The Pinkerton Agency also refused to submit its files, particularly those containing the names of its secret operatives.[96] When investigators insisted, Pinkerton employees purged the records. At the Detroit office, employees spirited company records out the back door while investigators served them with a subpoena at the front door.[97] Branch managers of the Burns Detective Agency engaged in a failed effort to destroy their records before subpoenas were served.[98] When investigators suspected that these files had been discarded, they dug through their trash bins and emerged with scraps of bills, receipts, and secret reports they painstakingly pieced back together. What they uncovered shocked the nation.[99] Even though La Follette was not surprised that "agencies purveying labor spies, [and] strikebreakers, . . . whose very business is founded on deceit, should attempt to conceal their activities," he was shocked to discover that "influential and respectable industrial corporations" like General Motors, which cleansed the files of firm president William S. Knudsen on two occasions, resorted to "such devices."[100] Many groped to justify their acts, including one executive, who, after admitting that he regularly hired spies, pleaded, "It's an employer's duty to know what his men are thinking about."[101]

In late March 1939, after nearly three years of hearings, La Follette and his co-chair Elbert D. Thomas introduced Senate Bill 1970, a tightly worded piece of legislation designed "to eliminate certain oppressive labor practices affecting interstate and foreign commerce." Also known as the Oppressive Labor Practices Act (OLPA), this bill prohibited industrial

Fig. 3.7 Hearing room of the Senate Committee on Education and Labor, September 25, 1936. Seated at the raised horseshoe desk, Senators Robert M. La Follette and Elbert D. Thomas interrogate Robert A. Pinkerton and general manager of the Pinkerton National Detective Agency Asher Rossetter regarding labor espionage and other violations of workers' civil liberties. © Bettmann/Corbis.

espionage, strikebreaking, the purchase and use of military-like arma-
ments, and the employment of private armed guards by industrialists
beyond their own premises.[102] Shortly after La Follette presented his
proposal to the Senate, Reuben T. Wood, a Democrat from Missouri,
introduced a similar bill in the House.[103] The opposition that the La
Follette–Thomas measure met as Congress began debate on the Oppressive Labor Practices Act (OLPA) evidences the gradual shift taken against
labor by the public and mirrored by Congress at the dawn of World War
II. With the rash of sit-down strikes, beginning in late 1936, and the
bloody jurisdictional battles between the AFL and the CIO the next year,
the public began to wonder if its sympathy toward organized labor had
been misplaced. In the House, Republican Clare E. Hoffman believed
that the La Follette committee "was more interested in disclosing the

Fig. 3.8 *United Mine Workers of America Journal* cartoon, published as the La Follette
committee uncovered the business community's reliance upon labor spies. May 1937.

violation of civil liberties on the part of employers than . . . on the part of strikers, labor organizers and unions."[104] Democrats, including one Senator who argued that the La Follette–Thomas proposal would "nationalize" labor by giving the federal government further control over industry's relationship with its workforce, joined in too.[105] As sharp as they may have been, these attacks proved less detrimental than the changing international situation. As German armies raced across northern Europe, the La Follette–Thomas bill became entangled in the growing debate over national defense.[106] Finally, in May 1940, after numerous changes, the Senate passed the La Follette–Thomas proposal by a vote of 34 to 20. Opposition in the House proved so strong that Wood could not muster enough votes to bring his companion measure to the floor.[107] La Follette, according to *Time* magazine, could have chosen "no worse time" to have introduced his act.[108]

While no sweeping federal legislation had been enacted, the revelations of the La Follette Committee sparked a strong public reaction against the anti-union industry. Cringing under an uncomplimentary light in April 1937, the Pinkerton board of directors unanimously agreed that "this agency in the future not furnish information to anyone concerning the lawful attempts of labor unions or employees to organize and bargain collectively."[109] "That is a phase of our business," Robert Pinkerton later told the *New York Times*, "that we are not particularly proud of and we're delighted we're out of it. However, there was nothing illegal about it at the time."[110] Abandoning what had been an important part of its business cost the Pinkerton Agency dearly as the agency's income dropped to an all-time low in the first full year after this announcement.[111] The following year the Corporations Auxiliary Company ended its labor discipline services.[112] In this environment espionage professionals like Harry Black of the Star Commissary and Employment Bureau found little work. "I haven't had a job since 1937, La Follette's investigation has cleaned out the business as far as I am concerned," he testified before the hearings on OLPA.[113] Many others, including Chester Brazier of the Railway Audit and Inspection Company, who noted that his employer's business had declined "tremendously because of the publicity and the fear of publicity," related similar stories.[114] For men like Harry Black and Chester Brazier things deteriorated further three years later when the National Association of Manufacturers denounced "the use of espionage, strikebreaking agencies, professional strikebreakers, armed guards, or munitions for the purpose of interfering with or destroying the legitimate rights of labor to self organization and collective bargaining."[115] By this time much of the business community came to realize that employing espionage services was not worth risking public condemnation.

After ten years of relative labor peace, the unprecedented strike violence of the Depression decade provided a bonanza for anti-union agencies. Although the purveyors of strikebreakers and professional armed guards found some work, the future belonged to those who offered more clandestine methods. While more overt forms of labor control often led to violence, the undercover operative or missionary was able to destroy unionization efforts without alarming the public. Moreover, shipping large bodies of men into strike areas was, after 1936, illegal. Ironically enough, this form of unionbusting finally came to an end with the dawning of an era in which employers demanded even greater subtlety in disciplining their workers. Following the La Follette hearings and the changes in the capital-labor relationship ushered in by the Wagner Act, a new breed of anti-union practitioners quickly responded to the changing needs of the business community.

4

THE UNIONBUSTING INDUSTRY SINCE THE WAGNER ACT

IN SPITE OF THE COOPERATION demonstrated by employers and workers as they struggled together to defeat fascism, once World War II ended, many businessmen moved aggressively to reestablish their dominance. As workers began to stir, strikes increased dramatically in the last months of the war and after VJ Day exploded in the greatest strike wave in American history. Although they had publicly renounced their dependence upon anti-union agencies after the La Follette committee hearings, many employers once again turned to outside specialists to discipline their workers.

As the economic environment changed, a new breed of unionbusting agencies—labor relations consultants—began offering their services to the business community. By operating within the bounds of an institutionalized capital-labor relationship, ushered in by the Wagner Act, these anti-union agencies provided an effective and subtle service for the next half-century. Armed with advanced degrees in industrial psychology, management, and labor law, their operatives carried briefcases rather than blackjacks as they manipulated not only the provisions of national labor law but also the emotions of those considering unionization. The services they offered continued to evolve, becoming more sophisticated and far more devious as these modern unionbusters skirted regulatory legislation. Motivated by the promise of a lucrative market, anti-union entrepreneurs once again demonstrated their ability to adapt to changing environments.

During the latter half of the 1940s a number of labor relations consulting firms, including Equitable Research Associates of New York, the Vincent J. Squillante Company, the Marshall Miller Company, and Labor Relations Associates, began offering a more sophisticated anti-union service to those employers who had not forgotten their opposition to collective bargaining.[1] Formed under the auspices of the Sears, Roebuck and Company in late 1939, Labor Relations Associates, the largest of these agencies, was led by this retail giant's head of employee relations, Nathan W. Shefferman.

The son of a prominent rabbi, he was born in 1887 in Baltimore and raised in Zanesville, Ohio. During the Depression he worked in radio and was known to New York listeners as "the Friendly Voice," an announcer who spoke on inspirational themes. Authoring a number of books on industrial relations, he also gained national recognition as an expert on labor matters. In 1933 he was picked as a member of the National Labor Board shortly after the establishment of that agency. His work in settling strikes eventually brought him an offer to work for Sears, Roebuck as the head of employee relations.[2] Far from an impartial mediator, Shefferman helped keep Sears stores and their suppliers union-free for the next two decades. For example, in 1956, his employees succeeded in ending the Retail Clerks Union's efforts to organize workers at seven Boston-area stores by employing tactics that Sears's vice-president for personnel, Walter Tudor, later described as "inexcusable, unnecessary and disgraceful."[3]

During the late 1940s, Labor Relations Associates expanded its operations beyond its parent company and their suppliers. With branch offices in New York and Detroit and a staff of thirty-five, by the middle of the next decade, many regarded Shefferman as the most successful unionbuster in the country. For nearly four hundred clients, including many small local employers, as well as large national concerns, such as the Whirlpool Corporation, his operatives set up anti-union employee groups called "Vote No" committees, designed ruses to uncover pro-union workers, and helped arrange "sweetheart" or "soft" contracts with friendly unions.[4] Many of these strategies had been perfected during countercampaigns conducted for Sears, Roebuck and Company. From 1949 through 1956, Shefferman's firm earned nearly $2.5 million in retainers and fees providing such services.[5]

During one three-year period ending in 1956, Whirlpool executives paid Labor Relations Associates more than $136,000 to keep three of its plants in the Midwest union-free.[6] Although they claimed to have hired this agency to test employees for flexibility and emotional stability, a "Master Plan" drawn up by one of Shefferman's chief operatives, and later uncovered in Whirlpool's files, provides insight into the tactics they employed at this manufacturer's plant in Clyde, Ohio. In this memo he wrote: "Find lawyer and guy who will set up a vote no committee, find leaders and sway them, go into local American Legion post and get material to turn over to vote no committee, give American Legion material we have and let vote no committee get it from them." He also encouraged Whirlpool officials to set up a "rotating committee," in which groups of workers vented their grievances and inadvertently exposed their union sympathies.[7] At Whirlpool's Marion, Ohio, plant, another operative set up a card file system in which he listed workers' feelings about the union. Many of those he regarded as pro-union lost their jobs. Using a "Human Equations Test" he also weeded out job applicants sympathetic to unionization.[8] Their efforts proved successful, for in early May 1956, Whirlpool employees overwhelmingly voted against the Machinists Union in an NLRB-sanctioned election.[9] Utilizing these and other more insidious ruses, Labor Relations Associates achieved the same results for other clients.

At the Morton Frozen Foods Company in Webster City, Iowa, two years earlier, Shefferman's agency not only ended a United Packing House Workers organization drive but also helped managers regain control over their employees. Shortly after arriving in this small town, two men in Shefferman's employ convinced a handful of Morton workers to set up an anti-union employee committee called "We the Morton Workers." Through this front group, members campaigned against the union and reported on those sympathetic to labor. One of the founders, Gary Long, claimed that he and a Labor Relations Associate representative "would go down through the list [of employees] and check off the ones we thought would vote yes, and the ones we thought would vote no."[10] While Long received a substantial pay increase as well as more opportunities for overtime, management fired those workers he listed as pro-union.[11] After they defeated the Packing House Workers union Shefferman's operatives arranged a "sweetheart contract" between the Morton organization and the Bakery and Confectionery Workers International Union of America, a union Morton managers could control. Drawing up this contract without an NLRB election, and without the participation of the workers, both parties signed the agreement in the office of Nathan W. Shefferman. He received more than twenty thousand dollars for his duplicity.[12]

Labor Relations Associates agents set up similar contracts for other companies, including the Ecko Products Company of Chicago and the Englander Company.[13] Many of these arrangements, like that with the latter firm, involved the International Brotherhood of Teamsters and their president, Dave Beck.

Shefferman first met Beck in the mid-1930s.[14] Realizing that Beck was an up-and-coming official in the Teamsters organization, Shefferman ingratiated himself with an endless flow of jokes and gags and soon became Beck's constant companion. As he hoped, this friendship opened up a number of business opportunities. Partners in deals ranging from supplying furniture for the new Teamsters building in Washington, D.C., to the sale of promotional toy trucks to Teamster locals, they reaped a fortune. Their anti-union schemes proved particularly profitable. While Shefferman built his reputation as a unionbuster, for his assistance in setting up "sweetheart" contracts, Beck received large cash gifts from Shefferman, including more than twenty-four thousand dollars during a two-year period ending in 1950.[15] It was this relationship, however, that eventually led to Shefferman's exposure before Congress and his undoing.

In the spring of 1957, as Shefferman and Beck's relationship flourished, Democratic senator John L. McClellan of Arkansas launched an inquiry into the activities of the United Textile Workers, Allied Industrial Workers, the Teamsters Union, and other national unions after a congressional investigation uncovered evidence that racketeers had infiltrated organized labor.[16] The Teamsters received the lion's share of scrutiny. As a fascinated public listened, a number of criminal characters, union members, and their leaders, including Beck and Jimmy Hoffa, testified to corruption and racketeering. Once Beck and Shefferman's dealings came to light, the senators looked into their relationship and the activities of Labor Relations Associates.[17] They called before Congress 145 employers who utilized their services and pored over this firm's records. Shefferman's ledgers revealed that he remained closely tied not only to the Teamsters union, but also to Sears, Roebuck and Company. During an eight-year period ending in 1956, for example, he purchased, at discount rates, nearly half a million dollars in merchandise from this retailer. Teamster leaders, including Beck, received the majority of these goods. He also spent thousands of dollars entertaining Teamster officials. This expense was also borne by Sears, Roebuck and Company.[18] Drawing upon Teamster funds, Shefferman also acted as Beck's agent, purchasing boats, nylon stockings, guns, a deep freeze, and socks, which Beck was unhappy with. "Tell them," he wrote to Shefferman, "their socks . . . are terrible, full of holes."[19] When called to the stand to explain these arrangements, Shefferman invoked the Fifth Amendment.[20]

Fig. 4.1 Appearing before the McClellan Hearings into union corruption, the founder of Labor Relations Associates, Nathan W. Shefferman, sidestepped questions regarding his firm's efforts to help its clients avoid bargaining collectively with their employees. AP/ Wide World Photos, 1957.

Before completing their investigation in early 1958, members of the McClellan committee submitted an interim report in which they demanded congressional action. Although much of their report dealt with union corruption, they made it clear that they were outraged by Shefferman's connections to the Teamsters and the myriad of anti-union ruses hatched by his agents.[21] Alarmed by the committee's belief that "the National Labor Relations Board [was] impotent to deal with Shefferman's type of activity," Congress sponsored a number of regulatory proposals, including the Landrum-Griffin Act, which President Eisenhower signed into law in the fall of 1959.[22] Also known as the Labor-Management Reporting and Disclosure Act (LMRDA), this bill required unions to "open their books" and mandated that businesses report to the secretary of labor any agreement with a labor relations consultant "where an objective thereof, directly or indirectly, is to persuade employees" in regards to their rights to bargain collectively. In addition, labor relations consultants were required to file an "Agreement and Activities Report" within thirty days after agreeing to persuade their client's employees to reject unionization.[23] At least for a few years the business community ended their dependence on firms like Labor Relations Associates.[24] Although he defended his labor relations career, releasing his side of the story in *The Man in the Middle* in 1961, the following year Shefferman closed his office in Chicago, the home base of his operations, and retired. Early in the winter of 1968 he passed away at the age of eighty-one.[25]

In less than a decade, the Landrum-Griffin Act would come to have little impact upon those who made their living breaking unions. While McClellan regarded this legislation as "far from adequate," Robert P. Griffin, who referred to the final enactment of the bill he coauthored as a "scissors and paste" job, believed it had been compromised in committee.[26] Less than five years after Eisenhower signed this legislation into law, the labor department weakened it further by requiring consultants to report their activities only after communicating *directly* to their client's workers.[27] Under this reading of the Landrum-Griffin Act, the Department of Labor took action against consulting agencies in only three cases since 1966, and between 1968 and 1974 "filed no actions at all."[28] This ruling provided the loophole anti-union practitioners like John Sheridan of John Sheridan and Associates needed. In the late 1970s, he said that his firm, like many labor consultants, did not file reports with

Fig. 4.2 Senator John McClellan's inquiry into the business community's reliance upon firms like Labor Relations Associates resulted in regulatory legislation. Copyright 1957 Time, Inc. Reprinted by permission.

the government since his agents did not speak directly to their clients' workers.[29] More important, men like Shefferman had given way to a new breed of unionbusters, like Sheridan. With degrees in industrial psychology, management, and labor law, they proved skilled at sidestepping not only the provisions of the National Labor Relations Act but also the guidelines of the LMRDA. Moreover, while their objectives differed little from their predecessors', their activities could be masked as constructive employee relations. The emergence of a pro-business environment around the same time created an environment conducive to breaking unions.

As anti-union practitioners came to fear the threat of exposure less and less and, by the 1970s, as the public came to look less critically upon the business community's efforts to avoid unionization, convinced workers were no longer the victims, "the number of consultants, and the scope and sophistication of their activities, . . . increased substantially," Assistant Secretary of Labor William Hopsgood reported at the end of that decade.[30] This assessment was corroborated by consultants like the founder of Modern Management Methods, Inc., Herbert G. Melnick, who testified in 1979 that he knew of a "dozen firms of substance" involved in labor consulting and that his industry had undergone a "tenfold growth in ten years."[31] Melnick, whose company reportedly assisted employers in 696 union organizing drives from 1977 to 1979, was most likely thinking of West Coast Industrial Relations Associates of California, which serviced 1,500 clients in one year, and John Sheridan, who once boasted that his outfit conducted representative election campaigns for hundreds of large companies.[32]

The many employers that turned to these mercenaries did so not only as a result of the dawning of a pro-business environment or because the government failed to enforce the management side of the LMRDA but because they provided an effective service. Even though there remain many reasons for the decline of the house of labor during the past two decades, one cannot discount the fact that, as "the number of consultants, and the scope and sophistication of their activities . . . increased substantially," unions began suffering increasing setbacks in NLRB-sponsored elections, members of the NLRB noted in 1980.[33] For example, while organized labor won 57 percent of all representative elections in 1970, within ten years this figure slipped to 46 percent. The number of decertification elections also increased more than three times around this period, with unions suffering defeat in 73 percent of these elections.[34] Modern Management Method's 93 percent winning ratio in NLRB elections from 1977 through 1979 evidences the destructive capabilities of one labor relations consulting firm.[35] Like many in this industry, Herbert Melnick claimed to sell a new vision of the workplace in which "the role of labor relations consultants is not to block union representation, but rather to help employers to . . . provide a safe and financially secure workplace for their employees."[36] Such paternalism fell far short, for many privately proved more interested in letting potential clients know—as did Ballew, Reinhardt, and Associates, Inc.—that "no client of ours who has used our service on a continued basis has ever been unionized."[37] In another example, Human Resources and Profits Associates, Inc., boasted in a circular letter in 1984: "Our 99% win rate is unmatched by any other law or management consulting firm in the world." Indeed, over 52 percent of their nine-hundred-plus election confrontations did not even go to an election because the union withdrew.[38]

The business community learned of the anti-union capabilities of labor relations consulting firms from the numerous seminars they began offering on union avoidance strategies during the 1970s.[39] In 1977, Executive Enterprises, Inc., doubled its program, holding its seminar, "How to Maintain Non-union Status," in a different city each month. "There is an upsurge in the number of companies that feel there are things they can do to maintain non-status," Lewis Abrams, president of this firm, claimed.[40] In another example, a major competitor of Executive Enterprises, AMR International, Inc., began holding its seminar three times a month during the latter part of the decade.[41] This firm, in addition to employing labor expert Charles Hughes, began publishing the *AMR Reporter*, a monthly anti-union newspaper.[42] In some cases, employer groups, such as the Hospital Association of New York, which brought in John Sheridan to speak to its members in 1980, served as intermediaries.[43]

For a fee ranging from $250 to $550, employers who attended these clinics picked up tips from specialists in industrial psychology and labor law and from onetime union men on the intricacies of employee relations programs that "make unions unnecessary."[44] "Any company that gets a union deserves it, and you deserve the one you get," Hughes, who provided his expertise to other consulting agents, told executives who

EXHIBIT
LONG'S RESPONSE TO SMITH'S LETTER

WEST COAST
INDUSTRIAL RELATIONS ASSOCIATION, INC.

August 16, 1976

Mr. Joel D. Smith, President
QUADCON INTERNATIONAL INCORPORATED
2444n Old Middlefield Way
Mountain View, CA. 94043

re: Employee Relations Services for Plant Start Up

Dear Joel:

Per your request, consider this our proposal to assist Quadcon
in its Southern California plant start up with the objective of
assisting you in developing policies and procedures that will
maintain non-union status and maximize your start up efficiency.
Our proposal covers a twelve month period from when we commence work.

A. Preparation of personnel policies, an   30 hours $1200.
    employee handbook and implementation
    of same.

B. Development of an employee orientation   30 hours $1200.
    program and implementation of same.

C. Development and implementation of a   40 hours $1600.
    wage and salary program for exempt and
    non-exempt personnel.

D. Development of selection criteria for   30 hours $1200.
    exempt and non-exempt personnel.

E. Recruiting and screening of initial   40 hours $1600.
    work force.

F. Supervisory training in sound employee   40 hours $1600.
    relations techniques for good morale
    and profit.

G. Miscellaneous matters connected with   16 hours $ 640.
    establishment of sound employee
    relations practices.
                                                             _____
        Total anticipated Cost (maximum) $9040.

Fig. 4.3   In a flyer for a 1979 seminar, West Coast Industrial Relations Associates promised expert counsel for firms facing union drives and for those whose employees wanted to initiate decertification proceedings. Without WCIRA's "specialized knowledge," company officials would be unable to "counter the thrust of aggressive labor unions." U.S. Congress, House of Representatives, Subcommittee on Labor Management Relations, Committee on Education and Labor, 96th Congress, 1st Session, Oversight Hearings (Washington: GPO, 1979).

Quadcon International Incorporated   Page 2

    The foregoing figures are predicated on your becoming members
of our Association and include the 10% membership discount. Your
membership fee would be $50.00 per month and you have a brochure on
membership services. A membership form is enclosed for your signa-
ture for your convenience.

    Since you are going about plant start up in a most intelligent
manner, and since we are damn good at what we do, we doubt you will
ever face a union organization attempt. However, assuming you did,
a plant of 100 to 200 employees would have counter-organizational
costs approximately as follows:

    A. Legal work connected with the   25 hours $1250
          National Labor Relations Board, to
          wit, RC petition, hearing and briefs.

    B. Conducting counter-organization   100 hours $4000.
          campaign.

                 Total Cost $5250.

    Hopefully your costs will be less than what we quoted as we'll
bill only for actual hours worked, but it is a pretty good ball park
figure based on our experience on similar assignments. I really
wouldn't worry about a non-union campaign for reasons already cited.
If you have any questions or would like more information you can
reach me at 415 969-8580.

                          Sincerely,

                          Fred R. Long, Esquire

FRL:mjt

Enclosure

bcc: Keil
      Geist
      Ross
      Rohan

attended a seminar offered by Executive Enterprises, Inc., in Atlanta in 1977. To avoid this burden he urged listeners to minimize sources of complaints union organizers could exploit. A company without disability coverage "only needs one horror case . . . to get everyone to sign a union card," he warned. In addition to hearing two lectures, "Attitude Survey Techniques for Measuring Union Sentiments" and "Specific Tools for Identifying Individual Values," these men and women received a "Communication Packet," which included sample letters crafted to persuade employees to reject unionization, and two books, *Making Unions Unnecessary* and *The Supervisor's Handbook on Maintaining Non-union Status,* both written by Hughes.[45] Other labor relations consultants proved more insidious. Convinced of African American workers' propensity to join unions, one consultant encouraged his listeners to hire only enough blacks to comply with Equal Employment Opportunity Commission regulations.[46] To New Jersey hospital executives John Sheridan advocated a more subtle approach by stressing the importance of "indoctrinating" new employees "into your philosophy, your program . . . before any union or malcontents can get their hands on that employee." To this end, he encouraged his listeners to draft a policy statement that made clear their company's opposition to unionization. He also went on to urge employers to screen applicants closely and to get rid of "anybody who is not . . . a team player."[47]

In those cases where preventive measures failed and workers demanded union representation, to those who paid to hear him discuss union avoidance, labor consultant Alfred DeMaria offered a host of tricks. For example, speaking for Executive Enterprises in Atlanta, he exhorted listeners to point out to their employees the union's "economic motives" for organizing. He also suggested that they mail pictures of striking workers at other plants or newspaper clippings detailing union scandals to these men and women.[48] Other consultants urged their clients to sidestep the law. At a seminar given by West Coast Industrial Relations Associates in Los Angeles in July of 1978, Fred Long told those in attendance that once a union filed a petition for an election, "you got at least sixty days to hire a hell of a lot of people you need to." He also provided advice on backdating payroll memoranda in order to grant a wage increase before an NLRB election and urged those facing a union drive to solicit grievances so as to "resolve all those problems . . . you can neatly resolve" before the election. "The probability is that you will never get caught. If you do ... the worst thing that can happen to you is that you get a second election and the employer wins ninety-six percent of those," he counseled those anxious about violating the law.[49]

Employers who attended these seminars heard labor experts tell them that, even if an election had not turned out favorably, or if their firms had been long unionized, all was not lost. John Sheridan often reminded his listeners that an election loss could be salvaged at the bargaining table. He told those who attended a seminar he sponsored in 1980 that good faith bargaining was such a vague term that management need only bargain and talk, not come to an agreement.[50] In addition to a host of labor lawyers, consulting agencies like Human Resources and Profits Associates, Inc., and Executive Enterprises, Inc., which held its seminar, "The Process of Decertification," in Atlanta and Ft. Lauderdale on a number of occasions in 1977 and 1978, also offered their clients instruction on the skills needed to decertify unions.[51] In Atlanta, those in attendance were told: "This meeting could make a big difference in the way you will be doing business a year from now."[52] In addition to leading employers through the intricacies of decertifying unions, other consultants, like James Baird, showed managers how to subtly encourage workers to initiate such procedures. Those attending a seminar sponsored by the Illinois State Chamber of Commerce in October 1978 heard him say, "It's a delicate question—how does someone else make [decertification] happen.... We'll talk about how to set it up so the employee comes in and asks all the important questions on his own."[53]

Whatever their method, these agencies proved successful in freeing their clients of union representation as an increasing number of decertification elections and union defeats in these contests paralleled the growth of the labor relations consulting business. In 1977, for example, employees at 1,794 workplaces called for such elections, a 188 percent increase over those numbers for 1967. In 76 percent of these elections, unions lost bargaining status, an 11 percent jump over the figures for the earlier year.[54] Finally, seminars provided consulting firms with the opportunity to inform potential customers of their other service: the orchestration of on-site anti-union campaigns.

Overwhelmed by the intricacies of national labor law and frightened by their employees' militancy, an increasing number of employers placed

---

ADVANCED MANAGEMENT RESEARCH
370 AVENUE OF THE AMERICAS · NEW YORK, N.Y. 10019 · 212-765-6400

John B. Grant
Division Manager

RE: MAINTAINING NON-UNION STATUS

Dear Fellow Executive:

- *Did you know that, even though your company provides competitive salaries and excellent working conditions, you may still present an irresistible target for union organizers this year?*

  Are you aware that, before a union organizer sets foot near your plant, he may know more about your company's strong and weak points than you know yourself?

  Did you know that unions love to come up against a company that's confident about its employees' loyalty—a company that's willing to let its record "speak for itself"—when the organizers come to call.

If there's one thing that's certain in this age of costly shortages, crippling strikes and rampant inflation —it's probably this: if your company or organization is non-union, it's in your best interest to *stay that way*.

We all realize that unionization can increase your operating costs — and headaches — dramatically. For example, a recent issue of *Boardroom Reports* stated that:

> "Labor costs in a union shop are between 25% and 35% higher than in a non-union shop. And that's not because of lower pay. It's because you don't have complex, debilitating work rules to conform to; you don't have to hire redundant workers; you don't have work stoppages, strikes or slowdowns."

Unfortunately, many executives seem to dwell in a "never-never-land" when it comes to labor unions. They believe that somehow, some way, if they just go on being "nice guys," the unions will forever stay away. Many are also totally unaware of the numerous, effective techniques that are available to ward off a union's encroachment. Still others mistakenly believe there is something "wrong"—or even worse, something "immoral"—about fighting to maintain non-union status.

For precisely these reasons, Advanced Management Research, one of America's leading management education institutions, created an entirely unique seminar for management. It's entitled

Fig. 4.4 Advanced Management Research advertised a three-day seminar—"Strategies for Preserving Non-union Status," presented by Charles L. Hughes—to prospective clients. Executives were promised a "no-holds barred look at the harsh realities of a union drive—one of the most difficult challenges" their companies would face. U.S. Congress, House of Representatives, Subcommittee on Labor Management Relations, Committee on Education and Labor, 96th Congress, 1st Session, Oversight Hearings (Washington: GPO, 1979).

STRATEGIES FOR PRESERVING NON-UNION STATUS and, quite frankly, we think it will be a landmark learning session—one of the most important seminars ever held for corporate managers . . .

STRATEGIES FOR PRESERVING NON-UNION STATUS will be led by a faculty team from the law firm of Jackson, Lewis, Schnitzler & Krupman. This team will be composed of partners and associates who have taken part in numerous seminars for trade and educational associations on the subject of maintaining non-union status, as well as other areas related to labor relations law. They will lecture and lead realistic, problem solving workshops to demonstrate management strategies and techniques.

The third day of the program will be led by Dr. Charles L. Hughes. A leader in the field of Labor Relations, Dr. Hughes has worked with numerous organizations in maintaining non-union status and assessing employee attitudes.

> You'll examine, for example, the preventive steps you can take to
> discourage a union from ever targeting your plant or organization . . . the
> ways to determine whether covert activity is taking place . . . how to react
> correctly when the organization drive comes out in the open . . . what to do
> if you're presented with a demand for immediate union recognition.

> You'll also find out what you can do to protect against unfair labor
> practices during the election campaign . . . how to investigate unions fully
> and fairly . . . how to prevent the signing of authorization cards based upon
> union misrepresentations . . . how to best give your side of the story to your
> employees . . . how to prepare for the election.

This practical seminar will also identify the many legal pitfalls that can trap even the most conscientious employer. You'll learn about simple, seemingly harmless mistakes that could void a successful election campaign and give "instant" recognition to the union. And you'll learn to avoid the all too common employer mistakes that swing employee sympathies to the side of the union.

STRATEGIES FOR PRESERVING NON-UNION STATUS is an exhaustive, no-holds barred look at the harsh realities of the unionization drive—one of the most difficult challenges your company faces today. All the subject matter will be explained in layman's terms, not "legalise"—and the case studies presented will be based upon *real corporate experiences*, not hypothetical situations.

We believe there has never been a seminar on the subject of labor relations as unique and thorough as this one. Naturally, we expect a very heavy enrollment. You can reserve your place now, however, by returning the registration coupon on the back of the enclosed brochure as soon as possible.

Better still, call us collect at (212) 765-6400. There is no need to send money now unless you wish. We'll be happy to bill you later. Thank you.

Most cordially,

John B. Grant
Division Manager

TD/nd

their trust in Modern Management Methods, Inc., West Coast Industrial Relations Associates, or one of hundreds of other consulting firms when facing an NLRB-sanctioned representative election. Joining with them for the duration of the battle, their agents assumed complete responsibility for their clients' countercampaigns, including planning corporate strategy from offices on location and commanding the company's entire human and financial resources.[55]

Although they claimed to tailor their strategy to each client's needs, most modern unionbusters employed a standardized three-pronged attack. Cognizant of LMRDA guidelines requiring consultants to report their activity only when engaged *directly* in persuading employees in regards to their right to bargain collectively, most consulting teams utilized supervisory personnel as "the critical link in the communications network."[56] To ensure their loyalty, they often coerced, cajoled, and threatened these men and women with the loss of their jobs.[57] "In any campaign where the issue is 'union or not?,' the one thing every supervisor should not be is 'non-committal,'" West Coast Industrial Relations Associates advised their clients.[58] Once a part of the anti-union team, front-line supervisors, like those at G.T.E. Lenkurt, Inc., "compiled and reported the names of union men and those sympathetic to unionization."[59] Questioning each employee repeatedly regarding his or her feelings about the union, front-line supervisors also enabled management's mercenaries to judge the effectiveness of their campaign and to design strategies to play upon each employee's reservations about unionization.[60]

Well aware of the power these men and women wielded, many consultants also utilized supervisory personnel to engage in "eyeball-to-eyeball communication" with their underlings.[61] For example, in the months before an NLRB election at the Pittsburgh Plate and Glass Company in Lexington, North Carolina, in 1979, consultants for Hogg, Allen, Ryce, and Blue of Coral Gables, Florida, required supervisors to "approach all the workers ... and ask them, weren't they man enough to speak for themselves, why did they need some outside third party to come in and do their talking for them?" Later each was "to give progress reports on the employees he tried to turn around in their thinking."[62] West Coast Industrial Relations Associates went so far as to provide their clients' supervisory staffs with a pamphlet outlining proven methods. In one section authors urged their clients' foremen to "analyze the employees (each employee separately, if possible) with whom you will be working to determine what points and arguments will most likely be telling . . . A supervisor likely can strike at least one responsive chord with every employee if he analyzes the situation carefully."[63] Often the pressure placed upon workers deepened as the election grew closer. In the days prior to a vote at St. Francis Hospital in Milwaukee in 1982, for example, the supervisors "created stress, pulled rank, cajoled, threatened, promised, personalized the issue and otherwise attempted to brain-wash the nurses."[64] If supervisory personnel could not be brought into the employer's camp, most consulting teams were not without other stratagems.

While union organizers' access to workers was easily limited, by controlling the shop floor employers enabled their allies to wage unremitting psychological warfare, bombarding workers, in some cases hour by hour, with posters, leaflets, personal letters, and speeches.[65] For example, during a countercampaign conducted at Mercy Hospital in Watertown, Massachusetts in the summer of 1980, operatives for Modern Management Methods, Inc., mailed letters to workers informing them of their right to work "without threats of strikes" or being forced to pay "union dues or fines."[66] On the other hand, consultants like Martin Levitt believed that "Thanksgiving, a time to be grateful for one's bounty," was the perfect time for distribution of his "count your blessings letter," in which he listed examples of management's largesse.[67] Others crafted management addresses, like the "captive audience" speech heard by workers at the Shelly and Anderson Furniture Company in 1972, which left workers with the impression that the company would go out of business if it lost the election.[68] While remaining within NLRA guidelines, these and other tricks created an environment far from what the NLRB described as ideal—one in which workers have the time to make free and rational decisions regarding unionization. In other, less obvious, ways, consultants manipulated national labor laws to achieve their ends.

Drafted in the 1930s when anti-union tactics proved far less subtle, the National Labor Relations Act, nearly half a century later, offered numerous opportunities for those skilled in labor law to circumvent its intent. Well aware of its shortcomings, one labor relations consultant referred to the NLRA as a "union buster's best friend."[69] Countercampaigns orchestrated by labor relations consultants, for example, often dragged on for extended periods, slowing the psychological momentum of an organizing drive while providing their clients with time to "massage" their workers. One common tactic called for management's negotiators to contest every nuance of an NLRB election. As one consultant put it, "even though a 'consent' election may be 'quicker' it has the same results as a shot in the head . . . always go to a hearing. It always works in your favor."[70] On behalf of his client, Harvey Rector filed numerous "patently frivolous" objections to delay an election requested by the International Union of Electrical Workers in 1970.[71] In another example, Gladys Selvin utilized a host of "delaying tactics" to discourage representatives of the Wholesale Delivery Drivers and Salesmen's Union from "seeking to bargain with" her client, West Coast Liquidators, Inc., the NLRB concluded in 1973.[72] Loosely constructed NLRA guidelines also allowed creative consultants, like John Sheridan, to change the size and character of the bargaining unit to their clients' advantage. In one instance, by convincing the NLRB that nurses at one client's facilities performed supervisory functions and were thus outside the bargaining unit, he won a campaign in which more than 90 percent of these women had signed union cards.[73]

While many proved skilled at stretching NLRA guidelines, other labor relations consulting firms paid little attention to national labor law. Hired by B.L.K. Steel to counter a unionization drive in 1979, West Coast Industrial Relations Associates, for instance, paid one client's employees to vote against the union, promised another a pay raise if the union lost, threatened others with the loss of benefits if the union won, and solicited grievances and interrogated workers. Although the NLRB documented these transgressions, this steel manufacturer's mercenaries avoided unfair labor charges handed down by that board.[74] In another case that year members of the NLRB issued thirty-eight complaints against St. Elizabeth's Hospital of Boston, while Modern Management Methods, Inc., the consulting team that orchestrated their campaign, escaped unscathed.[75] Both cases proved typical, for in the handful of times this board took legal action rarely did they issue penalties against management's consultants. Moreover, cognizant of the fact that when they penalized employers, the NLRB called for compensatory penalties rather than punitive measures, consulting agencies encouraged their clients to sidestep the law. Led to think in these terms, many employers inflicted irreparable damage to a union drive by firing one or two workers. While the NLRB often compelled them to rehire these workers and pay their back wages, to employers anxious to avoid paying union scale, such a strategy made economic sense.[76]

Nearly twenty years after President Eisenhower signed the Landrum-Griffin Act into law, Congress stumbled upon the business community's dependence upon this new breed of professional unionbusters when a House committee began hearing testimony on "the effects of modern workplace practices and strategies on individual workers."[77] Before what came to be known as the "Pressures in Today's Workplace" hearings nearly fifty people appeared, including union representatives, working people, academics, and representatives from two labor relations consulting firms. Lawmakers learned that little had changed since the enactment of the LMRDA. Although the consulting industry's spokesmen claimed that their firms acted only as industrial "marriage counselors," majority members rejected this contention, writing, "consultants promote a perspective of labor-management relations which exalts the short-run over the long-run, presuming that workers will vote against a union, if management exercises the correct combination of manipulation, persuasion and control during the relatively brief duration of an organizing campaign."[78] Much of the committee's interest centered on the business community and their mercenaries' reluctance to comply with the Landrum-Griffin Act.[79] Outraged by what they heard, they called for the Labor Department to "undertake a thorough re-examination of the reporting and disclosure provisions of the L.M.R.D.A." and even suggested that Congress "regard retention of the current statutory scheme as but one option."[80] Congress showed little interest in revamping the Landrum-Griffin Act.

The revelations of the "Pressures" hearings did, however, awaken the Labor Department to the extent and destructiveness of the anti-union industry and shook organized labor from its lethargy. During the last year of Jimmy Carter's administration the Department of Labor opened more than 330 new investigations into employer and consultant activity.[81] At the same time, organized labor launched a campaign to insure enforcement of this law and help workers counter the tactics employed by this new breed of unionbusters. In 1979, for example, the AFL-CIO's Department of Organizing and Field Services began issuing to labor organizers a special checklist to help them discover the presence of such agencies.[82] They also started keeping files on these firms and their tactics and disseminated this information through a monthly newspaper, *Report on Union Busters*.[83] At the grassroots level, union locals began picketing strike sites where labor consultants led anti-union campaigns, infiltrating labor relations consultants' seminars, and lobbying employers to end their dependence upon these mercenaries.[84] Their efforts paid dividends. In the spring of 1981, for example, the National Union of Hospital and Health Care Employees persuaded five hospitals in the Boston area to terminate their contract with Modern Management Methods, Inc.[85] Unfortunately, governmental efforts to end the business community's reliance upon these mercenaries proved short-lived.

With the election of a Republican president who made no secret of his determination to end regulations he believed restrained business, and as the public's hostility toward organized labor continued to mount, little came of the Labor Department's efforts to revitalize the Landrum-Griffin Act. The new administration not only showed little interest in pursuing those cases opened by Carter's labor administrators, but also went to great lengths to dismantle the management side of the LMRDA. For example, shortly after coming to office, Reagan's director of the Office of Labor-Management Standards Enforcement (LMSE), Richard G. Hunsucker, closed those LMRDA investigations opened under the previous administration, although he once acknowledged that anti-union management consultants "from everything I've read . . . would seem to

AFL-CIO · **Lane Kirkland**, *President* · **Thomas R. Donahue**, *Secretary-Treasurer* · 815 16th Street, N.W., Washington, D.C. 20006
Joseph Shantz, *Director of Organization and Field Services* · **Vincent O'Brien**, *Editor*

Fig. 4.5 By the late 1970s, as more employers turned to labor consulting firms to smash their workers' efforts to unionize, organized labor mounted a counteroffensive, detailing the tactics of such firms in a monthly newsletter. Reproduced courtesy of the AFL-CIO.

be on the increase."[86] In addition, while the LMSE office accorded the investigation of employer or consultant reporting cases equal priority to that given to union embezzlement complaints immediately after the "Pressures" hearings, "the L.M.S.E. Enforcement Strategy Document," issued during Reagan's first term, called for spending only 3 percent of the department's time on enforcing the management side of the LMRDA. In this environment, employers and their allies came to pay even less attention to the reporting provisions of the Landrum-Griffin Act.[87] In 1983, while more than seventy-one thousand union reports were submitted pursuant to LMRDA reporting requirements, only 198 consultants and employers filed reports. The Landrum-Griffin Act had become a dead letter, as the business community and its allies continued to "evade the spirit and sometimes the letter of federal law," concluded members of a House subcommittee in 1985.[88] Although these lawmakers echoed the demands of those who served on the "Pressures" inquiry, the 98th Congress, well aware of organized labor's declining popularity, showed little interest in either enhancing the powers of the LMRDA or ensuring its enforcement. In such a milieu the future looked bright for the business community's mercenaries. Reflecting on Reagan's landslide victory in 1984, one union official lamented at the AFL-CIO Executive Council meeting in February 1985, "the union-busters are in hog heaven now."[89]

Whereas previous investigations into unionbusting had prompted new generations of anti-union practitioners whose services proved subtler, in an environment that exalted the business community while according labor little sympathy, the newest wave of mercenaries felt free to resort to confrontational tactics. As unionbusting came full circle, men little different than the thugs employed by Bergoff or Farley would be once more in demand.

EPILOGUE

EMBOLDENED NOT ONLY BY the pro-business milieu of the Reagan years, but also by Congress's failure to regulate the activities of labor relations consulting firms, beginning in the mid-1980s and continuing into the new millennium, while some anti-union employers continued to rely upon the tactics of persuasion and manipulation, other beseiged firms launched blatantly aggressive campaigns. Although the general direction of professional unionbusting has been toward greater sublety, in an environment in which the public perceived organized labor no longer as a victim but as the aggressor, strike-bound employers felt safe turning to agencies that supplied replacement workers and professional security firms whose men proved to be little more than thugs. By the dawn of the twenty-first century, methods of unionbusting differed little from those of the first part of the twentieth century.

Ironically enough, business's renewed reliance upon professional strikebreakers, or, in their parlance, replacement workers, grew from the Supreme Court's ruling on labor's Magna Carta—the Wagner Act. After upholding the constitutionality of the National Labor Relations Act, the same justices ruled that companies could hire "permanent replacements" for strikers who walked out for "economic reasons."[1] Although few paid attention to this decision in 1938, by the last decade of the century William Gould, chairman of the NLRB, conceded that while the activities of agencies that provided strike-bound plants with replacement workers were far from "equitable or sensible," they remained "legal."[2] Until President Ronald Reagan brought in replacement workers to crush the air traffic controllers' strike in 1981, most employers, fearful of antagonizing the public, refrained from such tactics. With serious economic downturns in the middle of the 1970s and at the beginning of the 1980s, a growing army of permanently unemployed workers convinced managers of the utility of this strategy. Since the Professional Air Traffic Controllers' Organization's (PATCO) demise, the list of companies utilizing professional strikebreakers includes Eastern Airlines, Greyhound, Caterpillar, Hormel, Diamond Walnut, and the *Detroit Free Press* and the *Detroit News*.[3]

Manpower, Inc., the nation's largest employment agency, refuses to participate in strike work, but, as in the first part of the twentieth century when James A. Farley and Pearl Louis Bergoff enlisted thousands of men to take the place of striking workers, such armies are available to the employers. While private detective agencies once dominated the trade in strikebreakers, today employers turn to temporary employment agencies, like Worldwide Labor Support of Pascagoula, Mississippi, for such men. During a labor dispute at Caterpillar during the first part of the 1990s, while Worldwide provided two hundred welders, Manufacturing Technical Search, Inc., of Westchester, Illinois, and Strom Engineering Corporation, a temporary employment agency in Minnetonka, Minnesota, supplied this heavy-equipment manufacturer with replacement workers trained in other trades.[4] Other firms include BE&K, which maintains a data bank of the names of thousands of workers willing to cross picket lines, and Denver's U.S. Nursing Corporation.[5] In September of 1994, this latter firm demonstrated its capabilities by flying more than one hundred nurses to Port Jervis, New York, when caregivers went on strike at that city's Mercy Community Hospital. Each nurse received two to three thousand dollars per week and a per diem, as well as airfare.[6]

At the outset of the Detroit newspaper strike in the summer of 1995, newspaper executives contracted with Alternative Work Force (AWF) for six hundred replacement workers.[7] To protect the replacement workers they also hired Huffmaster Security, Inc., which supplied nearly five hundred armed guards. Although the spate of anti-Pinkerton laws that followed the Homestead debacle, the modernization of public police services, and the revelations of the La Follette hearings ended the business community's reliance on private police services, during the anti-union climate of the 1980s and 1990s employers like the *Detroit Free Press* and the *Detroit News* felt little apprehension when they turned to their late-twentieth-century equivalent: security specialists. After four months, the Detroit newspapers paid Huffmaster and Alternative Work Force $2.3 million for their services. Huffmaster, which sued the newspapers for $1.5 million more, was eventually replaced by the most notorious security specialists, Vance International's Asset Protection Team (APT).[8] Like their predecessors, security specialists employed plug-uglies not so much to guard private property as to intimidate and provoke strikers into acts of violence.

Fig. Epil. 1   In the mid-1990s, Vance guards battled with strikers during the Detroit Newspaper Strike. Strikers claimed the guards provoked them in order to secure an injunction. Copyright daymonjhartley.com. Reprinted by permission.

While earning the enmity of organized labor, Vance International's APT, like the Pinkerton Agency of the late nineteenth century, has reaped a fortune from the industrial conflict of the last fifteen years. Based in Oakton, Virginia, by 1996 this firm employed fifteen hundred people, their revenues reaching eighty-nine million dollars, a threefold increase from two years earlier. "Before we started, if you would have told me we would grow like this, I would never have believed you," Charles Vance, the founder of this firm once said.[9] Beginning his law enforcement career as a policeman for the city of Oakland, California, in the early 1960s Vance joined the Secret Service two years after graduating from the University of California at Berkeley, with a degree in criminology. The next decade found him serving on a White House security detail where he met and later married President Gerald Ford's daughter, Susan. He left this agency in 1979 and with two former Secret Service agents organized a private security firm, which, along with his marriage, failed in the early 1980s. He then struck out on his own, forming Vance International in 1984.[10]

After providing security consultation services for a Kentucky coal mining operation in the mid-1980s, he branched into strike work, organizing one of the many subsidiaries under the Vance International banner, the APT.[11] By the next decade, Vance could promise his clients, "Our tactical security teams ensure a safe operating environment for non-striking employees, replacement workers, corporate executives . . . [their] strong presence has neutralized many turbulent situations." He went on to boast that his guards come equipped with one thousand dollars worth of equipment and are trained in "non-confrontational security techniques, NLRB regulations, explosive identification, fire prevention, first aid and evidence gathering."[12] Since 1984 this subsidiary has worked more than six hundred strikes.[13] Although Vance executives reject the idea that their men are strike-busters, unionists argue that they differ little from their heirs: Pinkerton and Baldwin-Felts guards.

When the United Mine Workers of America (UMWA) staged a strike against the Massey Coal Company in the fall of 1984, Vance's Asset Protection Team demonstrated its ability to intimidate and provoke strikers. In addition to dispatching hundreds of guards armed with M-16s, shotguns, and pistols to the strike zones in West Virginia and Kentucky, Vance also supplied the mine operators with a sniping-countersniping expert. Well prepared to meet the hostility they knew their presence would spark, they wore riot helmets, shin guards, and body armor.[14] Although the mine owners insisted that they hired these guards to protect personnel and property, a number of impartial observers—including Virginia's secretary of state, Ken Hechler, who said that bringing in an outside security force "was like putting a spark to a tinder box"—questioned this assertion. He characterized Vance's men as "tough macho types who enjoy pushing people around. Out-of-state firms hire these people because they have records of excessive force." A reporter for the *Williamson (W. Va.) Daily News,* Mark Francis, agreed, claiming that "the security forces aggravated more violence than they prevented."[15]

Five years after the Massey dispute ended, when the Pittston Coal Company withdrew from its contractual obligation to provide health coverage to widows, pensioners, and disabled miners, Vance found his

Fig. Epil.2 Charles Vance, founder of Vance International's Asset Protection Team, argues that his firm provides only a protection service. Unionists see his men, involved in a number of strikes since the mid-1980s, as heirs of the Pinkerton or Baldwin-Felts agencies. Copyright Sam Kittner/kittner.com. Reprinted by permission.

APT involved in another hotly contested mining strike. While mine officials clamed to have hired their services to protect property and replacement workers it became apparent that their foremost objective was to intimidate and provoke the miners. Shortly after the miners walked out of the mines the tone of their countercampaign was established when a group of large and heavily armed APT men clad in blue jumpsuits, dark sunglasses, and combat boots made their appearance at the coal operator's biggest operation, McClure mine No. 1.[16] Atop one of the company's warehouses, guards erected a sniper's nest. As enraged strikers ambushed coal truck convoys escorted by gun-toting guards in Vance vehicles, the strike zone took on the appearances of a military

Fig. Epil.3 "Trigger," a sniper and counter-sniping expert brought in during the Massey Coal Strike in 1984 by Vance's Asset Protection Team. From *Soldier of Fortune Magazine*, September 8, 1986. Reprinted by permission.

engagement.[17] The outbreak of violence served Pittston well, for Vance's heavy-handed tactics were employed in conjunction with the use of "state-of-the-art equipment" (cameras and camcorders) to "document acts of violence or strike related incidents," enabling their clients to secure "restraining orders, injunctions, arbitration or criminal or civil actions."[18] Although Pittston spokeswoman Susan Copeland told reporters, "It has never been our intention to provoke anyone," unionists argued that the company's hired guns often instigated trouble in order to capture an incident on film.[19] "If they see you at the Piggly Wiggly, they'll pull out behind you. Sometimes they'll get in front of you and slow down and when you try to pass, they speed up just to agitate you," one miner's daughter complained.[20] Union leaders warned strikers: "They'll make obscene gestures to your family to provoke you and do things to lure you into court orders. Hold your cool."[21]

In eleven months of work around the Pittston mines APT cameramen shot miles of videotape and more than fifty thousand still photographs. Since a "good defense attorney can make an ill-prepared photographer confused and not very credible as a witness," photographers logged each in a personal notebook.[22] Vance guards also utilized infrared cameras to film strikers at night and deployed high-tech listening devices to eavesdrop on their conversations.[23] "Coupled with incident reports and testimony" this evidence resulted in sixty-four million dollars in fines levied against the UMWA in state courts and one million in federal court fines. "Although most of the fines were later forgiven," Vance boasted, "they helped to return the labor officials to the bargaining table."[24] Claiming to have led the way in the use of photo documentation equipment to discipline strikers, Vance told a reporter: "Having ten big tough-looking guys is far less effective than having one little guy with a camera."[25] The need for provocative displays of force—while an effective way to neutralize the impact of the strike as an economic weapon—proved this tactic's Achilles' heel.

In spite of the fear they inspired, the arrival of APT forces, like Pinkerton guards more than a century ago, often alienated the citizenry, invoked the wrath of local officials, and limited their effectiveness. Most residents of the strike zone regarded the men of these armies as gun thugs and mercenaries who were intent on disrupting the community and had little business in local affairs. While local citizens shunned the guards, law enforcement officials in Pike County, Kentucky, sympathetic with the miners' cause, or at least cognizant of their political clout, charged the Vance Agency with violating a county ordinance requiring private guards to establish county residency for a minimum of thirty days before being hired.[26] Partly because they disrupted the community by bringing in hired guns, Pittston lost the battle for community support and eventually the war. After nearly a year during which Pittston invested almost twenty million dollars on security and a fenced trailer park for the replacement workers, strikers and managers reached a tentative agreement favoring the strikers.[27]

More than a century after state legislators attempted to limit the activities of "Pinkerton" guards in the wake of the Homestead debacle, the provocative tactics employed by Vance's APT prompted lawmakers once again to address the issue of armies for hire. In 1997, after hearing that Vance guards ran union members off the road and videotaped them in their own backyards during the Detroit newspaper strike, lawmakers

Fig. Epil.4 Vance photographers during the Pittston Coal Strike of 1989. Vance claims to have led the way in recording union violence in order to help its clients win injunctions. Dickenson Star Photo, Clintwood, Virginia.

in the Michigan State House of Representatives enacted a bill governing the activities of agencies like Vance's APT.[28] Their bill failed in the upper house.[29] Years earlier, the state legislature in Minnesota approved a law restricting security guards to the property they were hired to protect. The bill's sponsor accused Vance guards of harassing strikers by stopping them on the highway and videotaping them in their homes during a strike at Boise-Cascade.[30]

Hard hit by the post-Reagan-era unionbusting tactics, within the last decade organized labor launched a two-pronged countercampaign. For those on the picket line, United Auto Workers officials, for example, urged their members not to be provoked by private guards and to "videotape in self defense."[31] Rather than just reacting to the tactics of security specialists union officials began filing grievances with the National Labor Relations Board. For example, during a strike at McDonnell Douglas in 1996, an officer of the International Association of Machinists charged: "You can't turn around without some guy in a Mission Impossible outfit [A.P.T. guard] shooting your picture. This is illegal intimidation and harassment of people exercising their legal right to strike, and we want it stopped."[32]

In 1992, with the promise of a sympathetic Democratic leadership, AFL-CIO leaders moved decisively, offering to limit their right to strike in return for a congressional ban on replacement workers. Introduced by Senator Robert Packwood of Oregon, labor's plan required both sides of a labor dispute to submit unresolved issues to a panel appointed by the Federal Mediation and Conciliation Service. Although this "change" in labor's "historic position" failed to generate congressional backing, that same year, Democratic presidential candidate Bill Clinton seized an issue of importance to working voters, pledging to ban the utilization of replacement workers during strikes.[33] As Clinton took office and newly appointed Secretary of Labor Robert Reich testified before a Senate Subcommittee on Labor that "the use of striker replacements is a vestige from an era that hopefully we are moving away from," Democrats enacted a bill the president would sign.[34] After it passed through the House, Republicans and conservative Democrats, believing the bill too broad, killed it in the upper house.[35]

Enraged over this defeat, as well as Clinton's endorsement of the North American Free Trade Agreement, AFL-CIO leaders informed the president that labor's support in his 1996 reelection campaign hinged on an executive order outlawing the use of such workers.[36] After Bridgestone-Firestone, Inc., hired 2,300 replacement workers during a rubber workers' walkout a year before the election, Clinton signed an executive order barring employers that utilized these mercenaries from obtaining federal contracts.[37] AFL-CIO president Lane Kirkland, who witnessed the signing, called it: "a welcome step towards justice in the workplace."[38] When a federal judge upheld the legality of the president's order in August of 1995, Reich told reporters that the decision was "a victory" not only for the president but "for working Americans."[39]

In the anti-union climate of the last decade modern anti-union practitioners remain free to practice their trade as regulatory legislative efforts have proven not only limited, but ineffective. In the last few years "APT has helped maintain operations during dozens of major strikes, as well as hundreds of small labor disputes," including a walkout at an Asarco, Inc., plant in Helena, Montana, in 1999.[40] Three years earlier APT agents intimidated, photographed, and compiled dossiers on striking employees during a UAW walkout at Caterpillar.[41] The following year they sent nearly thirty guards and photographers to Kansas City, Missouri, when steel workers struck against GST Steel Company.[42] Vance's APT is not the only security agency making money from the growing tensions between capital and labor. Executives of one of its major competitors, Special Response Corporation (SRC), based in Baltimore, Maryland, claim to have participated in a thousand labor disputes since the start of the decade. The company's advertisement—which features a uniformed agent holding a riot shield standing beneath a headline that reads, "A Private Army When you Need it Most"—promises prospective clients the security necessary to continue operations during a strike.[43] Through the World Wide Web this company also offers prospective clients a "guide for management . . . involved . . . in work stoppages and labor disputes."[44] Huffmaster Associates of Troy, Michigan, also continues to provide replacement workers and strike security services.[45] For instance, when workers walked off their jobs at the Pepsi bottling plant in Burnsville, Minnesota, in the summer of 2000, Huffmaster remained true to their firm's motto, "Keeping business in business," providing replacement workers and security services.[46] Temporary employment agencies—including U.S. Nursing Corporation, which provided five hundred nurses to St. Vincent's Hospital in Worcester, Massachusetts, when the

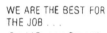

Fig. Epil.5 In the anti-union climate of the last two decades, a number of firms, including Special Response Corporation, have come to recognize the profits promised by labor unrest. Reprinted from *CovertAction Quarterly* no. 54 (fall 1995), Washington, D.C.

Massachusetts Nurses Association staged a walkout in early 2000—have also been little hampered by regulatory efforts. This army of medical professionals had earlier replaced striking nurses in New York, Rhode Island, and Washington.[47]

Agencies like Vance's APT, Huffmaster Associates, and U.S. Nursing Corporation are in a long line of commercial unionbusting agencies whose efforts enabled the American business community to avoid bargaining collectively with its workforce for more than a century. Gradual progressive change ushered in with the age of muckraking and reform and later the New Deal brought greater public tolerance for labor and eventually a place at the economic table. The success of the anti-union industry in the face of these changes lay in its practitioners' ability to devise new tactics to meet their clients' changing needs. The strategies they employed, which, until recently, continued to grow in sophistication and subtlety, reflected the public's slowly evolving sympathy for labor. During the past two or three decades, however, middle-class America's empathy for organized labor has begun to wane. During this period unionbusting has come to differ little from that practiced in the first part of the century. Given this industry's lengthy track record of adapting to new economic and social environments, there is every reason to believe that anti-union agencies will continue to capitalize on American employers' hostility toward bargaining collectively with their employees.

NOTES

Introduction

1. Nothing has been written on professional armed guard or strikebreaking agencies, and only a handful of scholars have studied the impact that labor spies have had on unionization efforts. See Gary M. Fink, "Labor Espionage: The Fulton Bag and Cotton Mills Strike of 1914–1915," *Labor's Heritage* 1 (Apr. 1989): 29; Gary M. Fink, *The Fulton Bag and Cotton Mills Strike of 1914–1915: Espionage, Labor Conflict, and New South Industrial Relations* (Ithaca: ILR Press, 1993); Charles K. Hyde, "Undercover and Underground: Labor Spies and Mine Management in the Early Twentieth Century," *Business History Review* 60 (spring 1986): 1–27; Rhodri Jeffreys-Jones, "Profit Over Class: A Study in America Espionage," *Journal of American Studies* 6 (1972): 238–48.

2. William E. Fulmer, "When Employees Want to Oust their Union," *Harvard Business Review* 56 (Mar.–Apr. 1978), 164; Anne Lawrence and John Williams, "Union Busters and the Law: Consultants and Employer Non-compliance with the Reporting Requirements of the Landrum-Griffin Act in California," research paper completed for the Center for Labor Research and Education Institute of Industrial Relations, University of California at Berkley, quoted in U.S. Congress, House of Representatives, Report of the Subcommittee on Labor Management Relations of the Committee on Education and Labor, *The Forgotten Law: Disclosure of Consultant and Employer Activity Under the L.M.R.D.A.*, 98th Congress, 2nd Session (1985). Even the authors of the two most important studies of the labor movement in the twentieth century, James R. Green and Robert Zieger, fail to mention the use of professional anti-union agencies when explaining organized labor's decline since World War II. See James R. Green, *The World of the Worker: Labor in Twentieth-Century America* (New York: Hill and Wang, 1980); Robert Zieger, *American Workers, American Unions* (Baltimore: Johns Hopkins University Press, 1986).

3. United States Industrial Commission on Labor Legislation, *Final Report of the Industrial Commission,* vol. 19 (Washington, D.C.: Government Printing Office, 1902), 891–92.

4. "The Strike-breakers," *Independent* 17 (Oct. 1901), 2456.

5. Edward Levinson, *I Break Strikes! The Technique of Pearl L. Bergoff* (New York: Robert M. McBride and Company, 1935; rpt., New York: Arno and New York Times, 1969), plate #5.

6. Although the handful of scholars who have studied industrial espionage negate the destructive abilities of these agencies, a wealth of evidence points in a much different direction. Gary M. Fink argues that although undercover operatives supplied by the Railway Audit and Inspection Company caused union leaders no end of trouble during a strike directed against the Fulton Bag and Cotton Mill Company in Atlanta in 1914–15, their efforts were not crucial in the defeat of the strike. Charles Hyde's study of the Quincy Mining Company's use of outside espionage services led him to the conclusion that spies failed to perform anti-union functions with much success. British author Rhodri Jeffreys-Jones suggests that their mercenary motives rendered these agencies ineffective in breaking strikes. See Gary M. Fink, "Labor Espionage"; Charles K. Hyde, "Undercover and Underground"; Rhodri Jeffreys-Jones, "Profit Over Class"; U.S. Congress, Senate, Subcommittee of the Committee on Education and Labor, 75th Congress, 2nd Session, 1937, *Industrial Espionage.*

Chapter One

1. Rhodri Jeffreys-Jones, *Violence and Reform in American History* (New York: New Viewpoints, 1978), 86.

2. Frank Morn, *The Eye that Never Sleeps: A History of the Pinkerton National Detective Agency* (Bloomington: Indiana University Press, 1982), 97.

3. James D. Horan, *The Pinkertons: The Detective Dynasty that Made History* (New York: Crown Publishers, 1967), 2.

4. Morn, *Eye that Never Sleeps,* 19.

5. Horan, *Pinkertons,* 14

6. Allan Pinkerton, *Professional Thieves and the Detective* (New York: G. W. Carleton and Company, 1880), 1–54.

7. Ibid., 24–25.

8. Ibid.

9. Morn, *Eye that Never Sleeps,* 19–23.

10. Horan, *Pinkertons,* 23.

11. Ibid., 25.

12. U.S. Congress, Senate, 52nd Congress, 2nd Session, S. Report #1280, "Investigation of Labor Troubles at Homestead," (1893), 49 (hereafter cited as Senate Report #1280).

13. Allan Pinkerton, *Strikers, Communists, Tramps, and Detectives* (New York: G. W. Carleton and Company, 1878), x–xi.

14. "Strikes and Lockouts," *Sixteenth Annual Report of the Commissioner of Labor, 1901* (Washington, D.C.: Government Printing Office), 803–6.

15. Morn, *Eye that Never Sleeps,* 99.

16. Ibid., 97; Senate Report #1280, 52–59, 242–43.

17. *Workingman's Advocate,* June 20, 1874; *Chicago Tribune,* June 22, 1874; *Chicago Times,* July 28, 29, 1874.

18. *Workingman's Advocate,* June 20, 1874; *Chicago Times,* July 29, 1874; *Chicago Tribune,* June 22, 1874.

19. *Workingman's Advocate,* July 25, 1874.

20. Herbert G. Gutman, "The Braidwood Lockout of 1874," *Journal of the Illinois State Historical Society* 53 (1960): 18–19.

21. Morn, *Eye that Never Sleeps,* 98.

22. Ibid., 93.

23. *Hocking Sentinel,* July 17, 1884, 3.

24. Henry Spurrier to Governor George Hoadly, July 14, 1884, and Elias Boudinot to Hoadly, July 14, 1884, papers of Governor George Hoadly, 1884–86, MS Collection #314, The Ohio Historical Society, Columbus, Ohio; *New York Times,* July 16, 1884; Andrew Birtles, "Governor George Hoadly's Use of the Ohio National Guard in the Hocking Valley Coal Strike of 1884," *Ohio History* 91 (1982): 52.

25. *Columbus Daily Times,* July 21, 25, 1884, 1

26. Birtles, "Governor Hoadly's Use," 52.

27. Robert Ozanne, *A Century of Labor-Management Relations at McCormick and International Harvester* (Madison: University of Wisconsin Press, 1967), 16.

28. *New York Times,* Apr. 10, 1886, 2.

29. Ibid., Oct. 9, 1886, 1, and Oct. 11, 1886, 5.

30. *Chicago Daily News,* Oct. 18, 1886.

31. *New York Times,* Oct. 17, 1886, 2.

32. *Chicago Daily News,* Oct. 21, 1886.

33. *Chicago Tribune,* Oct. 9, 1886.

34. Quoted in Louise Carroll Wade, *Chicago's Pride: The Stockyards, Packingtown, and Environs in the Nineteenth Century* (Urbana: University of Illinois Press, 1987), 248.

35. Wade, *Chicago's Pride,* 248.

36. Harry J. Carmen, Henry David, and Paul N. Guthrie, eds., *The Path I Trod: The Autobiography of Terrence V. Powderly* (New York: Columbia University Press, 1940), 149, 154.

37. *New York Times,* Oct. 20, 1886, 3; *Chicago Daily News,* Oct. 20, 1886; U.S. Congress, House of Representatives, 52 Congress, 1st Session, House Report #2447 (1892), "Investigation of the Employment of Pinkerton Men" (hereafter cited as House Report #2447), 214.

38. *New York Times,* Nov. 9, 1886, 1.

39. *Chicago Times,* Feb. 3, 1887; *Chicago Tribune,* Apr. 22, 1887; *Journal of the House of Representatives of the Thirty-Sixth General Assembly of the State of Illinois* (Springfield, Ill.: State Printing Office, 1889), 137, 349–50.

40. *Chicago Tribune,* Sept. 7, 1888.

41. July 17, 1887.

42. "Pinkerton's Men," *Nation,* Jan. 27, 1887, 70.

43. *New York Times,* Jan. 19, 1887, 8.

44. *Jersey City Evening Journal,* Jan. 18, 1887.

45. Ibid., Jan. 19, 20, 1887; *New York Times,* Jan. 20, 1887.

46. *Jersey City Evening Journal,* Jan. 20, 1887; *Irish World,* Jan. 29, 1887.

47. *Jersey City Evening Journal,* Jan. 21, 1887; *Irish World,* Jan. 29, 1887.

48. *Newark Evening News,* Jan. 21, 1887, 1; *Irish World,* Jan. 29, 1887.

49. *New York Times,* Jan. 26, 1887; *Jersey City Evening Journal,* Jan. 24, 1887; *Jersey City Argus,* Feb. 2, 1887.

50. *New York Times,* Jan. 23, 1887; Charles F. Peck, *Fifth Annual Report of the Bureau of Statistics of Labor for the Year 1887,* Assembly Document No. 47 (Albany, 1888), 342–45.

51. *New York Times,* Jan. 26, 1887; *Jersey City Evening Journal,* Jan. 24, 1887; *Jersey City Argus,* Feb. 2, 1887.

52. "Pinkerton's Men," 70.

53. *Newark Evening News,* Jan. 22, 1887.

54. *New York Times,* Jan. 22, 1887; *Jersey City Argus,* Jan. 24, 1887; *Jersey City Evening Journal,* Jan. 25, 1887.

55. *Knights of Labor,* Oct. 30, 1886, 5.

56. Frank Drew, "The Present Farmers' Movement," *Political Science Quarterly* 6 (June 1891): 301; *Knights of Labor,* Aug. 4, 1888, 7.

57. U.S. Congress, *Congressional Record,* 52nd Congress, 1st Session (1893) 23: 4223, 4225, pt. 5.

58. Ibid., 4225.

59. House Report #2447, 36.

60. Horan, *Pinkertons,* 344.

61. Ibid., 343–44.

62. House Report #2447, ix.

63. Sigmund Spaeth, *Weep Some More My Lady* (Garden City, N.Y.: n.p., 1927), 235–36, quoted in Philip S. Foner, *Labor Songs of the Nineteenth Century* (Urbana: University of Illinois Press, 1975), 244.

64. *Journal of the Knights of Labor,* July 7, 1892, 1.

65. House Report #2447, 1–2.

66. Ibid., ii.

67. Horan, *Pinkertons,* 352–53.

68. House Report #2447, 190, 192.

69. Quoted in Leon Wolf, *Lockout: The Story of the Homestead Strike of 1892: A Study of Violence, Unionism, and the Carnegie Steel Empire* (New York: Harper and Row, 1965), 156.

70. House Report #2447, xiv.

71. Ibid.

72. Senate Report #1280, 1.

73. Ibid., 94–105, 47–60.

74. Ibid., 129.

75. Ibid., xv.

76. House Report #2447, xi.

77. Ibid., xiii.

78. Ibid., views of Buchanan xxviii, Stockdale lxviii; *Congressional Record*, 52nd Congress, 1st Session, 23: 6418; Act of March 3, 1893, ch. 208 sec 1, 27 stat. 591 (5 U.S.C. 53, 1934).

79. House Report #2447, xvi.

80. Senate Report #1280, 227.

81. *Sixteenth Annual Report of the Commission on Labor* vol. 16 (Washington, D.C.: Government Printing Office, 1901), 992–1033; Henry Warrum, *Peace Officers and Detectives: The Law of Sheriffs, Constables, Marshalls, Municipal Police, and Detectives* (Greenfield, Ind.: William Mitchell, 1895), 106–13.

82. For a summary of such laws see *Sixteenth Annual Report of the Commission on Labor* 16:992–1033.

83. State of Illinois, Legislature, *House Journal* (1893), 52.

84. State of Illinois, *Laws of 1893*, 129.

85. *Laws of the Commonwealth of Pennsylvania Passed in the Session of 1893* (Harrisburg: E. K. Meyers, State Printer, 1893), 174–75; J. Barnard Hogg, "Public Reaction to Pinkertonism and the Labor Question," *Pennsylvania History* 11 (1944): 180.

86. U.S. Congress, Senate, Subcommittee of the Committee on Education and Labor, *Strikebreaking Services*, S. Report 6, pt. 1, 76th Congress, 1st Session, 1939, 16 (hereafter cited as *Strikebreaking Services*).

87. *Sixteenth Annual Report of the Commissioner of Labor*, 16:992.

88. Quoted in Horan, *Pinkertons*, 357.

89. *New York Times*, Aug. 17, 1892; *New York World*, Aug. 18, 1890; "Unity and No Surrender," *Journal of the Knights of Labor* 11 (Aug. 1890): 2.

90. Senate Report #1280, 19.

91. Ibid., 18.

92. Morn, *Eye that Never Sleeps*, 102.

93. Senate Report #1280, 24–30.

94. Ibid., 32.

95. Ibid., 79.

96. Ibid., 81.

97. U.S. Congress, Senate, Committee on Education and Labor, *Conditions in the Paint Creek District West Virginia*, Hearings pursuant to Senate Resolution #37, 63rd Congress, 1st Session, 1913 (Washington, D.C.: Government Printing Office, 1913), 869 (hereafter cited as *Conditions in Paint Creek District*).

98. Howard B. Lee, *Bloodletting in Appalachia: The Story of West Virginia's Four Major Mine Wars and Other Thrilling Incidents of Its Coal Fields* (Morgantown: West Virginia University Press, 1969), 190.

99. Richard M. Hadsell and William E. Coffee, "From Law and Order to Class Warfare: Baldwin-Felts Detectives in the Southern West Virginia Coal Fields," *West Virginia History* 40 (spring 1979), 270–71.

100. Hadsell and Coffee, "Law and Order," 272.

101. David Alan Corbin, *Life, Work, and Rebellion in the Coal Fields: The Southern West Virginia Miners, 1880–1922* (Urbana: University of Illinois Press, 1981), 50.

102. R. V. Hennen and D. D. Teets Jr., *Fayette County* (Wheeling: Wheeling News Litho Company, 1919), 21–29.

103. Evelyn Harris and Frank Krebs, *From Humble Beginnings: West Virginia State Federation of Labor, 1903–1957* (Charleston: West Virginia Labor History Publishing Fund, 1960), 58.

104. "Report," *United Mine Workers Journal,* Nov. 21, 1909.

105. Quoted in Hadsell and Coffee, "Law and Order," 278.

106. U.S. Coal Commission, *Report of the U.S. Coal Commission* (Washington, D.C.: Government Printing Office, 1923), 411.

107. Harris and Krebs, *From Humble Beginnings,* 73; Howard B. Lee, *Bloodletting,* 17.

108. Lee, *Bloodletting,* 20; *United Mine Workers Journal,* Jan. 16, 1913, 1; *United Mine Workers Journal,* Mar. 13, 1913, 1–3.

109. Lee, *Bloodletting,* 20.

110. Ibid., 21.

111. Ibid., 24.

112. Harold E. West, "Civil War in the West Virginia Coal Mines," *Survey,* Apr. 5, 1913, 43–45; Fred Mooney, *Struggle in the Coal Fields: The Autobiography of Fred Mooney* (Morgantown: West Virginia University Library, 1967), 76.

113. Ralph Chaplin, *When the Leaves Come Out and Other Rebel Verses* (Cleveland: published by the author, 1917), 31.

114. Hadsell and Coffee, "Law and Order," 281.

115. *Charleston Daily Mail,* July 26, 1912.

116. Ibid., 280; Lee, *Bloodletting,* 29–30; *Conditions in the Paint Creek District,* 1:846–47, 964–65.

117. Ibid.; Lee, *Bloodletting,* 38–40.

118. Lee, *Bloodletting,* 38–39; *Conditions in the Paint Creek District,* 1:640–42.

119. *New York Call,* June 21, 1913.

120. Lawrence R. Lynch, "The West Virginia Coal Strike," *Political Science Quarterly* 39 (December 1914), 640; *Conditions in the Paint Creek District,* 1:396.

121. West Virginia Legislature, *Acts,* 1913, 173–74.

122. Committee on Coal and Civil Liberties, "Coal and Civil Liberties, Report to the U.S. Coal Commission" (report submitted Aug. 11, 1923), U.S. Department of Labor Library, Washington, D.C., 14–20.

123. U.S. Commission on Industrial Relations, *Final Report and Testimony of the Commission on Industrial Relations* (Washington, D.C.: Government Printing Office, 1916), vol. VII, 6439 (hereafter cited as *CIR Hearings*); George S. McGovern and Leonard F. Guttridge, *The Great Coalfield War* (Boston: Houghton, Mifflin Company, 1972), 74–75.

124. *CIR Hearings,* vol. VII, 6397.

125. *CIR Hearings,* vol. VIII, 7296; Zeese Papanikolas, *Buried Unsung: Louis Tikas and the Ludlow Massacre* (Salt Lake City: University of Utah Press, 1982), 46, 69.

126. McGovern and Guttridge, *The Great Coalfield War,* 179.

127. *CIR Hearings,* vol. VII, 6397.

128. *Trinidad Chronicle-News,* August 18, 1913.

129. U.S. Commission on Industrial Relations, *Report on the Colorado Strike*, 5; *CIR Hearings*, vol. VII, 6597.

130. *Rocky Mountain News*, September 12, 1913.

131. *CIR Hearings*, VII, 6950.

132. *CIR Hearings*, vol. VII, 6527; 6562–63.

133. *CIR Hearings*, vol. VII, 6563, 6449; U.S. Congress, House of Representatives, 63rd Congress, 3rd Session, House Document No. 1630, *Report on the Colorado Strike Investigation* (Washington, D.C.: Governement Printing Office, 1915), 37 (hereafter cited as *Colorado Strike Investigation*).

134. U.S. Commission on Industrial Relations, *Report on the Colorado Strike*, 102; Walter Fink, *The Ludlow Massacre* (Denver: Williamson-Haffner Publishers, 1915), 92, in *Massacre at Ludlow: Four Reports*, edited by Leon Stein and Philip Taft (New York: Arno and New York Times, 1971).

135. Papanikolas, *Buried Unsung*, 90; *Rocky Mountain News*, October 17, 1913.

136. *CIR Hearings*, vol. VIII, 7065; *Rocky Mountain News*, October 18, 1913.

137. *Colorado Strike Investigation*, 17.

138. *Rocky Mountain News*, October 18, 1913.

139. *Rocky Mountain News*, November 21, 1913; *Trinidad Chronicle-News*, November 21, 1913; Colorado Adjunct General's Office, *The Military Occupation of the Coal Strike Zone of Colorado, by the Colorado National Guard, 1913–1914: Report of the Commanding General to the Governor, Colorado, 1914* (Denver: Press of the Smith-Brooks Printing Company, 1914), 16–17.

140. Papanikolas, *Buried Unsung*, 122.

141. Max Eastmen, "Class War in Colorado," *The Masses* (June 1914), 7.

142. *Colorado Strike Investigation*, 6; Elias M. Ammons to John Chase, November 17, 1913, Ammons Papers, Division of State Archives, Denver, Colorado.

143. Elias M. Ammons to John Chase, November 17, 1913, Ammons Papers, Division of State Archives, Denver, Colorado.

144. West, *Report on the Colorado Strike*, 132.

145. McGovern and Guttridge, *The Great Coalfield War*, 261.

146. McGovern and Guttridge, *The Great Coalfield War*, 288.

147. U.S. Congress, Senate, Committee on Education and Labor, Hearings pursuant to S. 80, to Investigate Recent Acts of Violence in the Coal Fields of West Virginia, 67th Congress, 1st Session, 1921–22, 1:115–24, 159; 2:892–93 (hereafter cited as *West Virginia Coal Fields Hearings*).

148. *West Virginia Coal Fields Hearings*, 1:212.

149. Ibid., 206–7, 209–10, 216–17; *Charleston Gazette*, May 21, 1929, 7; *West Virginia Coal Field Hearings*, 1:205–12, 382–86, 487–90, 2:881–905.

150. Quoted in Lon Savage, *Thunder in the Mountains: The West Virginia Mine Wars, 1920–1921* (Pittsburgh: University of Pittsburgh Press, 1990), 43.

151. *Bluefield Daily Telegram*, May 20, 21, 1920.

152. Lee, *Bloodletting*, 56.

153. Ibid., 56–64. The short film *Smilin' Sid* is no longer available. It is rumored that

coal operators stole the last copy. *The Labor Films Guide* (<http://www.nathannewman.org/ EDIN.labor/.resource/.films.html>).

154. *United Mine Workers Journal,* July 1, 1920, 8–9.

155. *West Virginia Coal Fields Hearings,* 1:115–23.

156. Lee, *Bloodletting,* 59–60.

157. Savage, *Thunder in the Mountains,* 44.

158. Ibid., 46–47.

159. Lee, *Bloodletting,* 62; Savage, *Thunder in the Mountains,* 49.

160. Richard D. Lunt, *Law and Order vs. the Miners: West Virginia, 1907–1933* (Hamden, Conn.: Archon, 1979), 146.

161. Corbin, *Life, Work, and Rebellion in the Coal Fields,* 215; *Indianapolis Times,* Feb. 11, 1921.

162. Mooney, *Struggle in the Coal Fields,* 87.

163. *Wheeling Intelligencer,* Aug. 2, 1921.

164. *West Virginia Coal Fields Hearings,* 738–39.

165. *United Mine Workers Journal,* Aug. 15, 1921; Lee, *Bloodletting,* 68.

166. Lee, *Bloodletting,* 68, 191.

167. Lee, *Bloodletting,* 70; *Parkersburg Sentinel,* Dec. 19, 1921, 1.

168. *New York Times,* Aug. 7, 1921, 18.

169. Quoted in Hadsell and Coffee, "Law and Order," 283.

170. Lee, *Bloodletting,* 65.

171. Joseph Willits, "The Conclusions and Recommendations of the U.S. Coal Commission as to Labor Relations in Bituminous Coal Mining," *Annals of the American Academy of Political Science* 3 (1924): 97–109.

172. Quoted in Hadsell and Coffee, "Law and Order," 284.

173. Ibid.

174. Phil M. Conley, *Life in a West Virginia Coal Field* (Charleston: American Constitutional Association, 1923), 48.

Chapter Two

1. F. B. McQuiston, "The Strike-Breakers," *The Independent* (October 17, 1901), 2456–57.

2. Ibid.

3. B. T. Fredricks, "James Farley, Strike-breaker," *Leslie's Magazine* 59 (May 1905): 105.

4. *Plattsburgh (N. Y.) Daily Press,* Mar. 18, 1905, 1; Leroy Scott, "'Strikebreaking' as a New Occupation," *World's Work* 10 (May 1905): 6200.

5. Edward Levinson, *I Break Strikes! The Technique of Pearl L. Bergoff* (New York: Robert M. McBride and Company, 1935; rpt., New York: Arno and the New York Times, 1969), 30.

6. *New York Times,* Sept. 11, 1913, 1.

7. Leroy Scott, "'Strikebreaking,'" *World's Work* 10 (May 1905): 6200.

8. Levinson, *I Break Strikes,* 31.

9. For a discussion of local support for carmen see Scott Molloy, *Trolley Wars: Streetcar Workers on the Line* (Washington, D.C.: Smithsonian Institution Press, 1996).

10. Edward Levinson "The Right to Break Strikes," *Current History* 45 (Feb. 1937): 81.

11. Edwin E. Witte, *The Government in Labor Disputes* (New York: Arno and New York Times, 1969), 209n.

12. "Industrial Policing and Espionage," *Harvard Law Review* 52 (Mar. 1939): 798.

13. Quoted in Levinson, *I Break Strikes*, 31.

14. Quoted in Phillip S. Foner, *History of the Labor Movement in the United States: The Policies and Practices of the American Federation of Labor, 1900–1909* (New York: International Publishers, 1964), 45.

15. Levinson, *I Break Strikes*, 30.

16. *New York Times*, Sept. 11, 1904, 1.

17. Scott, "'Strikebreaking,'" 6200.

18. *Providence Evening Telegram*, June 4, 1902.

19. Paul Buhle, Scott Molloy, and Gail Sansbury, eds., *A History of Rhode Island Working People* (Providence: Regine Printing Company, 1983), 31–32.

20. *Providence Journal*, June 6, 1902.

21. Buhle, Molloy, and Sansbury, *History*, 31–32.

22. *New York Times*, July 6, 1902, 3; Buhle, Molloy, and Sansbury, *History*, 31–32.

23. Gregg D. Kimball, "The Working People of Richmond: Life and Labor in an Industrial City, 1865–1920," *Labor's Heritage* 3, no. 2 (Apr. 1991): 56.

24. Fredricks, "James Farley, Strike-breaker," 106; *New York Times*, Sept. 11, 1904, 1.

25. *New York Times*, Sept. 11, 1904, 1

26. Scott, "'Strikebreaking,'" 6201.

27. *New York Times*, Sept. 11, 1904, 7.

28. Ibid., 1.

29. Ibid., 7.

30. Foner, *Policies and Practices*, 106, 103; *New York Times*, Sept. 6, 1904, 2.

31. *New York Times*, Sept. 11, 1904, 1.

32. Foner, *Policies and Practices*, 104; Fredricks, "James Farley, Strike-breaker," 106; *New York Times*, Mar. 3, 1905, 1.

33. Scott, "'Strikebreaking,'" 6200.

34. Ibid., 6201–3.

35. *New York Times*, Mar. 3, 1905, 1.

36. Scott, "'Strikebreaking,'" 6201.

37. Ibid.

38. William Brown Meloney, "Strikebreaking as a Profession," *Public Opinion* 38 (Mar. 1905): 441.

39. *Plattsburgh (N.Y.) Daily Press*, Mar. 18, 1905, 1.

40. Fredricks, "James Farley, Strike-breaker," 106; Scott, "'Strikebreaking,'" 6199–200.

41. Scott, "'Strikebreaking,'" 6200.

42. *New York Times*, Mar. 17, 1905, 2.

43. Meloney, "Strikebreaking as a Profession," 441.

44. *New York Herald,* Mar. 3, 1909, 3

45. Scott, "'Strikebreaking,'" 6202.

46. Ibid., 6203.

47. Meloney, "Strikebreaking as a Profession," 441.

48. Foner, *Policies and Practices,* 104.

49. *New York Times,* Mar. 17, 1905, 2.

50. Ibid., Mar. 3, 1905, 1.

51. Ibid., Aug. 12, 1913, 1.

52. Foner, *Policies and Practices,* 104.

53. Howard B. Myers, "The Policing of Labor Disputes in Chicago," Ph.D. diss., University of Chicago, 1929, 594.

54. *Chicago Tribune,* May 3, 1905.

55. *Chicago American,* May 7, 1905.

56. *Chicago Examiner,* May 2, 1905.

57. Myers, "Policing," 585.

58. Meloney, "Strikebreaking as a Profession," 441.

59. *New York Times,* Mar. 7, 1905, 1; Sept. 11, 1904, 1.

60. *Richmond Times-Dispatch,* June 17, 1903, 1; *New York Herald,* quoted in *American Industries* 3 (Apr. 1905): 3.

61. *Plattsburgh (N. Y.) Daily Press,* Mar. 18, 1905, 1.

62. Levinson, *I Break Strikes,* 29–30, 32.

63. John H. Graige, "The Professional Strikebreaker," *Collier's Weekly,* Dec. 3, 1910, 20.

64. Fredricks, "James Farley, Strike-breaker," 109, 108.

65. Graige, "Professional Strikebreaker," 20; Rhodri Jeffreys-Jones, *Violence and Reform in American History* (New York: New Viewpoints, 1978), 81.

66. Meloney, "Strikebreaking as a Profession," 441.

67. *Adirondack News,* Dec. 29, 1906, 1.

68. *Plattsburgh (N. Y.) Sentinel,* May 10, 1907.

69. Fredricks, "James Farley, Strike-breaker," 108–9.

70. Frank Morn, *The Eye that Never Sleeps: A History of the Pinkerton National Detective Agency* (Bloomington: Indiana University Press, 1982), 166.

71. *San Francisco Examiner,* May 3, 1907, 1.

72. Michael Kazin, *Barons of Labor: The San Francisco Building Trades and Union Power in the Progressive Era* (Urbana: University of Illinois Press, 1987), 134.

73. *San Francisco Bulletin,* May 18, 1907.

74. John H. Graige, "The Violent Art of Strikebreaking," *Collier's Weekly,* Jan. 7, 1911, 29.

75. *Argonaut,* Aug. 8, 1904.

76. Robert E. L. Knight, *Industrial Relations in the San Francisco Bay Area, 1900–1918* (Berkeley: University of California Press, 1960), 186.

77. *San Francisco Examiner,* May 6, 1907, 1.

78. John Bernard McCloin, *San Francisco: The Story of a City* (San Rafael, Calif.: Presidio Press, 1978), 281–82.

79. Henry K. Brent, "The Strike Situation in San Francisco," *Street Railway Journal* 30, no. 12 (Sept. 21, 1907): 417–18.

80. *San Francisco Chronicle,* May 7, 8, 1907.

81. *New York Times,* May 8, 1907, 1; *San Francisco Chronicle,* May 8, 1907.

82. *San Francisco Chronicle,* May 8, 1907.

83. *New York Times,* May 8, 1907, 1.

84. *San Francisco Bulletin,* May 18, 1907; *San Francisco Chronicle,* May 8, 1907.

85. *New York Times,* May 9, 1907, 8.

86. Ibid., May 8, 1907, 1.

87. Ibid., May 10, 1907, 5.

88. Ibid., May 9, 1907, 1.

89. *San Francisco Examiner,* May 13, 1907, 1–2; *Electric Railway Review,* May 18, 1907, 658.

90. *New York Times,* May 26, 1907, 3.

91. Walton Bean, *Boss Ruef's San Francisco: The Story of the Union Labor Party, Big Business, and the Graft Prosecution* (Berkeley: University of California Press, 1967), 242.

92. *New York Times,* June 3, 1907, 8.

93. *Argonaut,* July 6, 1907.

94. *San Francisco Chronicle,* Aug. 7, 10, 1907.

95. "Farley Breaks up Strikebreakers Camp," *American Federationist* 15 (Feb. 1908), 116–17.

96. Morn, *Eye That Never Sleeps,* 166.

97. Not only was Farley portrayed as a legitimate ally to the business community, his activities and opinions were frequently reported in local papers. During the New York traction strike, Farley was hailed as "the man who developed the business into a science," and his picture appeared on a number of occasions in the *New York Herald* (Sept. 11, 1904, 6, 3; Sept. 6, 1904, 3; Mar. 3, 1905, 3). After one man was killed in the reckless operation of a subway car, this newspaper reported a growing anger against imported strikebreakers and stopped writing about Farley's activities and opinions (*New York Herald,* Mar. 4, 1905, 3).

98. Levinson, *I Break Strikes,* 32.

99. *New York Times,* Sept. 11, 1913, 1.

100. Ibid.

101. Stephen J. Leonard, "Bloody August: The Denver Tramway Strike of 1920," *Colorado Heritage* (summer 1995): 18–31; Levinson, *I Break Strikes.*

102. W. P. Mangold, "On the Labor Front," *New Republic,* Oct. 3, 1934, 213.

103. Edward Levinson, "Strikebreaking Incorporated," *Harper's Magazine,* Nov. 1937, 724.

104. Levinson, *I Break Strikes,* 120.

105. Mangold, "On the Labor Front," 213.

106. *New York Times,* Aug. 13, 1947, 5; Levinson, *I Break Strikes,* 35–36.

107. "Strikebreaking," *Fortune,* Jan. 1935, 58; *New York Post,* Oct. 25, 1934, 1.

108. Levinson, *I Break Strikes,* 36; Albert E. Kahn, *High Treason: The Plot Against the People* (New York: Lear Publishers, 1950), 133.

109. "Strikebreaking," 58.

110. *New York Post,* Oct. 25, 1934, 1.

111. *New York Herald,* June 29, 1907, 3; *New York Tribune,* June 29, 1907, 1.

112. *New York Herald,* June 27, 1907, 3.

113. *New York Evening World,* June 29, 1907, 1.

114. *New York Times,* June 30, 1907, 1.

115. Quoted in Levinson, *I Break Strikes,* 46–47.

116. "Strikebreaking," 59.

117. Ibid.; *New York Call,* July 16, 1909, 1; Paul U. Kellogg, "The McKees Rocks Strike," *Survey,* Aug. 7, 1909, 656–57; *New York Tribune,* July 16, 1909, 1.

118. *New York Call,* July 16, 1909, 1; Kellogg, "McKees Rocks Strike," 656–57; *New York Tribune,* July 16, 1909, 1.

119. *New York Call,* July 16, 1909, 1; Kellogg, "McKees Rocks Strike," 656–57; *New York Tribune,* July 16, 1909, 1.

120. Quoted in Levinson, *I Break Strikes,* 71.

121. *New York Post,* Oct. 24, 1934, 6.

122. Quoted in Mangold, "On the Labor Front," 213.

123. *New York Times,* Aug. 28, 1909, 2.

124. *New York Post,* Oct. 24, 1934, 6.

125. *New York Times,* Aug. 29, 1909, 1.

126. Ibid., Aug. 28, 1909, 2.

127. *Peonage in Western Pennsylvania,* Hearings before the Committee on Labor of the House of Representatives, 62nd Congress, 1st Session, Aug. 1, 1911 (Washington, D.C.: G.P.O., 1911), 89.

128. *New York Times,* Aug. 28, 1909, 2.

129. Ibid., July 15, 1909, 1.

130. Ibid., Aug. 26, 1909, 2.

131. *Pittsburgh Leader,* Aug. 13–15, 1909, 1.

132. John Ingham, "A Strike in the Progressive Era: McKees Rocks, 1909," *Pennsylvania Magazine of History and Biography* 90, no. 3 (July 1966): 366.

133. *New York Times,* Aug. 29, 1909, 1; *Peonage in Western Pennsylvania,* 3–4; *Pittsburgh Leader,* Aug. 22, 1909, 1.

134. See testimony of L. J. Carroll, *Peonage in Western Pennsylvania,* 103.

135. Ibid., 7.

136. *New York Post,* Oct. 24, 1934, 6.

137. Ibid.

138. *Peonage in Western Pennsylvania,* 7.

139. *New York Times,* Aug. 28, 1909, 2; *Peonage in Western Pennsylvania,* 13.

140. *New York Times,* Aug. 29, 1909, 2.

141. Ibid.

142. *Pittsburgh Leader,* Aug. 23, 1909, 1.

143. Ibid., Sept. 1–3, 1909, 1.

144. *New York Sun,* Aug. 29, 1909, 1.

145. Louis Duchez, "Victory at McKees Rocks," *International Socialist Review*, Oct. 1909, 290; Rufus Smith, "Some Phases of the McKees Rocks Strike," *Survey*, Oct. 2, 1909, 41.

146. Kahn, *High Treason*, 137n.

147. "Strikebreaking," 60.

148. *New York Post*, Oct. 25, 1934, 6.

149. Hamilton Basso, "Strike-Buster: Man Among Men," *New Republic*, Dec. 12, 1934, 125.

150. *New York Post*, Oct. 24, 1934, 1.

151. "Strikebreaking," 89.

152. *New York Post*, Oct. 25, 1934, 6.

153. "Strikebreaking," 57.

154. For background on the CIR see Graham Adams, *Age of Industrial Violence, The Activities and Findings of the United States Commission on Industrial Relations, 1910–15* (New York: Columbia University Press, 1966); Valerie Jean Conner, *The National War Labor Board* (Chapel Hill: University of North Carolina Press, 1983), 12–18; Joseph A. McCartin, *Labor's Great War* (Chapel Hill: University of North Carolina Press, 1997), 12–37.

155. John R. Commons, *Myself* (Madison: University of Wisconsin Press, 1964), 166–67, quoted in Melvyn Dubofsky, "Abortive Reform: The Wilson Administration and Organized Labor, 1913–1920," in James E. Cronin and Carmen Siriann, eds., *Work, Community, and Power* (Philadelphia: Temple University Press, 1983), 205.

156. U.S. Commission on Industrial Relations, *Final Report of the Commission on Industrial Relations* (Washington, D.C.: Barnard and Miller, 1915), 71 (hereafter cited as *Final Report*).

157. Ibid., 145.

158. Ibid.

159. Ibid., 355.

160. Leonard Rappaport, "The United States Commission on Industrial Relations" (M.A. thesis, George Washington University, 1957), 2.

161. U.S. Congress, Senate, 63rd Congress, 2nd Session, Senate Document #381, *Report on the Strike in the Copper Mining District of Michigan*, 1914, 59.

162. Levinson, *I Break Strikes*, 130–32.

163. *Survey*, July 31, 1915, 387; *New Republic*, Aug. 14, 1915, 38–39; [Jersey City] *Jersey Journal*, July 20–21, 1915; George Dorsey, "The Bayonne Refinery Strike of 1915–1916," *Polish American Studies* 33 (1976): 23.

164. *Bayonne (New Jersey) Evening Review*, May 2, 1913, 10, 15, 18, 22, 23.

165. John A. DeBrizzi, "The Standard Oil Strikes in Bayonne, New Jersey, 1915–16," *New Jersey History* 101 (1983), 2; Foner, *History of the Labor Movement in the United States: On the Eve of America's Entrance into World War I, 1915–1916* (New York: International Publishers, 1982), 44.

166. Gladys M. Sinclair, *Bayonne Old and New: The City of Diversified Industry* (New York: Marantha Publishers, 1940), 85–86.

167. Levinson, *I Break Strikes*, 220; Sinclair, *Bayonne Old and New*, 174.

168. *Wilkes-Barre Record*, October 27, 1915, 1.

169. *Wilkes-Barre Times-Leader*, November 1, 1915, 1.

170. Ibid., Nov. 2, 1915, 1.

171. Harold Cox, "The Wilkes-Barre Street Railway Strike of 1915," *Pennsylvania Magazine of History and Biography* 94 (1970): 82–83.

172. Ibid.

173. Cox, "Wilkes-Barre," 83.

174. "Wilkes-Barre Strike Settled," *Electric Railway Journal* 48 (December 23, 1916), 1312–13.

175. Levinson, *I Break Strikes*, 214–16.

176. *Kansas City Post*, Aug. 7, 1917, 1; *Kansas City Star*, Aug. 11, 1917, 2.

177. *Kansas City Post*, Aug. 11, 1917, 1.

178. Ibid., 2; *Kansas City Star*, Aug. 11, 1917, 1.

179. *Kansas City Star*, Aug. 14, 1917, 2; *Kansas City Times*, Dec. 12, 1958, 52.

180. *Kansas City Post*, Aug. 16, 1917, 1.

181. "Strikebreaking," 57.

182. *New York Times*, Sept. 2, 1920, 1.

183. Ibid., Apr. 25, 1922, 3.

184. Foster Rhea Dulles and Melvyn Dubofsky, *Labor in America: A History* (Arlington Heights, Ill.: Harlan Davidson, 1984), 244.

185. "Strikebreaking," 60–61.

186. Levinson, *I Break Strikes*, 231.

187. *New York Post*, Oct. 25, 1934, 6.

188. Levinson, *I Break Strikes*, 232.

189. Irving Bernstein, *The Lean Years: A History of the American Worker, 1919–1929* (Boston: Houghton, Mifflin Co., 1960), 90; James R. Green, *The World of the Worker: Labor in Twentieth-Century America* (New York: Hill and Wang, 1980), 143.

190. "Strikebreaking," 92, 56.

191. Ibid., 56.

192. Levinson, *I Break Strikes*, 268–72.

193. Ibid.

194. Ibid., 290.

195. "Strikebreaking," 92; Thomas W. Gavett, *Development of the Labor Movement in Milwaukee* (Madison: University of Wisconsin Press, 1965), 155.

196. Basso, "Strike Buster," 81; *New Republic*, Dec. 12, 1934, 124–26.

197. "Strikebreaking," 92.

198. Kahn, *High Treason*, 139.

199. NLRB (1937), 670; U.S. Congress, Senate, Subcommittee of the Committee on Education and Labor, "Hearings pursuant to Senate Resolution 266," *Violations of Free Speech and Rights of Labor*, 74–76th Congress, 1936–1939, pt. 18, exhibit 3861, 7972 (hereafter cited as *La Follette Hearings*).

200. *Tonawanda (N.Y.) Evening News*, Mar. 8, 1937.

201. NLRB (1937), 672; *La Follette Hearings*, pt. 18, exhibit 3861, 7973.

202. National Labor Relations Board, *Decisions and Orders of the National Labor Relations*

Board, 2:671; Robert B. B. Brooks, *When Labor Organizes* (New Haven: Yale University Press, 1938), 141; *Strikebreaking Services,* 121.

203. National Labor Relations Board, *Decisions and Orders,* 2:703.

204. Ibid.

205. Brooks, *When Labor Organizes,* 141–42.

206. National Labor Relations Board, *Decisions and Orders of the National Labor Relations Board,* 2:705; *New York Times,* Nov. 25, 1936, 13.

207. *Strikebreaking Services,* 118; NLRB (1937), 632; *La Follette Hearings,* pt. 18, exhibit 3861, 7961–62.

208. *Strikebreaking Services,* 117.

209. 74th Congress, 1933–35, 2nd Session, Senate Report no. 1420, 1.

210. 74th Congress, 1933–35, House Report no. 2431, 1.

211. *Congressional Record,* 74th Congress, 2nd Session, 10219; *Strikebreaking Services,* 117.

212. *Strikebreaking Services,* 127; D. S., "Industrial Spying in Trade Unions," *Workers Age,* Jan. 1938, 8.

213. Levinson, *I Break Strikes,* 281–82, 307.

Chapter Three

1. *Strikebreaking Services,* 23, 25.

2. Ibid., 25.

3. U.S. Congress, Senate, Committee on Education and Labor, 74th Congress, 2nd Session, *Hearings on 266* (Washington, D.C.: Government Printing Office, 1936), 48–49, 60–66, 70–72 (hereafter cited as *Hearings on 266*). U.S. Congress, Senate, Committee on Education and Labor, *Hearings on S. 1970,* 76th Congress, 1st Session, 1939, 14 (hereafter cited as *Hearings on S. 1970*).

4. Morn, *The Eye that Never Sleeps: A History of the Pinkerton National Detective Agency* (Bloomington: Indiana University Press, 1982), 62–63.

5. Allan Pinkerton, *Tests on Passenger Conductors Made by the National Police Agency* (Chicago: George H. Fergus, 1867), 4–5.

6. Letter from George Bangs to Allan Pinkerton, Dec. 2, 1872, Pinkerton papers, Library of Congress, Washington, D.C.

7. Letter from Allan Pinkerton to William Pinkerton, Dec. 2, 1872, Pinkerton papers, Library of Congress, Washington, D.C.

8. Morn, *Eye That Never Sleeps,* 63.

9. Ibid., 93.

10. May 9, 1889.

11. Morris Friedman, *The Pinkerton Labor Spy* (New York: Wilshire Book Co., 1907), 4.

12. Donald L. McMurry, *The Great Burlington Strike of 1888: A Case History in Labor Relations* (Cambridge, Mass.: Harvard University Press, 1956), 182, 178.

13. Morn, *Eye that Never Sleeps,* 98.

14. T. A. Rickard, *A History of American Mining* (New York: McGraw-Hill, 1932), 327–28.

15. Charles A. Siringo, *Two Evilisms: Pinkertonism and Anarchism* (Austin, Tex.: Steck-Vaughn Company, 1968), 37; Charles A. Siringo, *Rita and Spurs: The Story of a Lifetime Spent in the Saddle as a Cowboy Detective* (New York: Haughton Mifflin Company, 1927), 159.

16. Charles A. Siringo, *A Cowboy Detective: A True Story of Twenty-Two Years With a World-Famous Detective Agency* (Chicago: W. B. Conkey, 1912; rpt., Lincoln: University of Nebraska Press, 1988), 137–38.

17. Ibid., 141–42.

18. Siringo, *Rita and Spurs*, 163–64.

19. Ibid., 159.

20. Siringo, *Cowboy Detective*, 137–38.

21. Siringo, *Rita and Spurs*, 164; Orlan Sawey, *Siringo* (Boston: Twayne Publishers, 1981), 108.

22. Siringo, *Rita and Spurs*, 172.

23. *Spokane Review*, July 13, 1892.

24. Richard E. Lingenfelter, *The Hardrock Miners: A History of the Labor Mining Movement in the American West, 1863–1893* (Berkeley: University of California Press, 1974), 208–9.

25. Siringo, *Cowboy Detective*, 178.

26. Sawey, *Siringo*, 111.

27. Vernon H. Jensen, *Heritage of Conflict: Labor Relations in the Nonferrous Metals Industry up to 1930* (Ithaca: Cornell University Press, 1950), 55.

28. E. H. Murphy to J. H. McGill, President, J. H. McGill Manufacturing Company, Valparaiso, Ind., Aug. 16, 1920. Joseph Labadie Collection, University of Michigan Graduate Library, Ann Arbor, quoted in Rhodri Jeffreys-Jones, *Violence and Reform in American History* (New York: New Viewpoints, 1978), 110.

29. "The Culprits Cry 'Stop Thief!'" *American Federationist*, Jan. 1904, 35.

30. Commonwealth of Massachusetts, *Proceedings of the Twenty-sixth Annual Convention of the Massachusetts State Board of the AFL* (1911), 92–93.

31. Kelcher to J. B. Furnas, General Food Products Company, New York, July 22, 1920, letter on file with the Joseph Labadie Collection, University of Michigan Graduate Library, Ann Arbor.

32. Jeffreys-Jones, *Violence and Reform in American History*, 105.

33. Ibid.

34. J. F. McNames, "Spies and Traitors," *Brotherhood of Locomotive Firemen and Engineer's Magazine* 46 (Feb. 1909): 449–52.

35. W. D. Haywood, *A Detective* (n.d., n.p.), Joseph Labadie Collection, University of Michigan Graduate Library, Ann Arbor.

36. Friedman, *Pinkerton Labor Spy*, 64.

37. Ibid., 64.

38. Ibid., 28–38.

39. Edwin E. Witte, *The Government in Labor Disputes* (New York: McGraw-Hill Book Company, 1932; rpt. New York: Arno and New York Times, 1969), 182. For insight into industrial espionage during the Progressive era see Gary Fink, *The Fulton Bag and Cotton*

Mills Strike of 1914–15: Espionage, Labor Conflict, and New South Industrial Relations (Ithaca N.Y.: ILR Press, 1993).

40. Quoted in U.S. Congress, Senate, Committee on Education and Labor, *Labor Policies of Employer's Associations, The National Association of Manufacturers*, S. Report #6, pt. 6, 76th Congress, 1st Session, 1939, 12.

41. J. H. Smith to W. Hamper, Oct. 10, 1906, enclosure in W. Hamper to Samuel Gompers, Oct. 12, 1906, Quoted in the American Federation of Labor Records, the Samuel Gompers, reel 63, item 254.

42. J. E. Spielman, *The Stool Pigeon and the Open Shop Movement* (Minneapolis: American Publishing Co., 1923), 142–43.

43. The Interchurch World Movement, *The Commission of Inquiry, Report on Steel Strike of 1919* (New York: Harcourt, Brace and Company, 1920), 21, and *Public Opinion and the Steel Strike: Supplementary Reports of the Investigators to the Commission of Inquiry* (New York: Harcourt, Brace and Company, 1921), 2.

44. Quoted in Jermiah Patrick Shalloo, *Private Police: With a Special Reference to Pennsylvania* (Philadelphia: American Academy of Political and Social Science, 1933), 182.

45. Quoted in Interchurch World Movement, *Public Opinion and the Steel Strike*, 56.

46. Interchurch World Movement, *Public Opinion and the Steel Strike*, 5.

47. Ibid., 28.

48. U.S. Congress, Senate, Committee on Education and Labor, *Industrial Espionage*, S. Report No. 46, pt. 3, 75th Congress, 2nd Session, 1937, 2, 22 (hereafter cited as *Industrial Espionage*).

49. *Hearings on 266*, 69.

50. *Hearings on S. 1970*, 17.

51. Ibid.

52. Irving Bernstein, *The Turbulent Years: A History of the American Worker* (Boston: Houghton Mifflin Company, 1970), 517.

53. U.S. Congress, Senate, Subcommittee of the Committee on Education and Labor, Hearings pursuant to Senate Res. 266, *Violations of Free Speech and Rights of Labor*, 74th–76th Congress, 1936–1939, pt. 2, exhibit 317, 676 (hereafter cited as *La Follette Hearings*).

54. *Hearings on S. 1970*, 14.

55. *Industrial Espionage*, 26; *La Follette Hearings*, pt. 15, exhibit 2792.

56. *Hearings on S. 1970*, 15.

57. Leo Huberman, *The Labor Spy Racket* (New York: Modern Age Books, 1937), 23–24.

58. *La Follette Hearings*, pt. 8, exhibit 2843.

59. *Industrial Espionage*, 62.

60. Ibid., 38; *La Follette Hearings*, pt. 6, 2098.

61. See *La Follette Hearings*, pt. 6, 2462, for Pinkerton hooking activities.

62. Beulah Amidon, "Employers and the Spy Business," *Survey Graphic*, May 1937, 266; *La Follette Hearings*, pt. 1, 42–43.

63. Amidon, "Employers and the Spy Business," 266; *La Follette Hearings*, pt. 1, 42–43.

64. *La Follette Hearings*, pt. 1, 105.

65. Ibid., pt. 1, 13 and 41–47, for Railway, Audit, and Inspection Company; pt. 2, 501, 562, and pt. 6, 2462, for Pinkerton hooking activities; pt. 4, 1150–51, 1378–79, for Corporations

Auxiliary Company; pt. 8, 2821–22, for hooking by Burns Agency operatives; Gordon Hopkins, "The Labor Spy," *Social Action,* June 15, 1937, 4.

66. *Industrial Espionage,* 39.

67. *La Follette Hearings,* pt. 5, 1538.

68. *Industrial Espionage,* 28; *Hearings on S. 1970,* 15; *La Follette Hearings,* pt. 15, exhibit 2791.

69. *Industrial Espionage,* 67; *La Follette Hearings,* pt. 5, 1616.

70. *La Follette Hearings,* pt. 5, 1458; *Industrial Espionage,* 63.

71. *La Follette Hearings,* pt. 4, 1313–16.

72. *Hearings on S. 1970,* 17.

73. National Labor Relations Board, *Decisions and Orders of the National Labor Relations Board* (Washington, D.C.: Government Printing Office, 1938), 9:546; *Industrial Espionage,* 57.

74. National Labor Relations Board, *First Annual Report of the National Labor Relations Board* (Washington, D.C.: Government Printing Office, 1936), 75.

75. *La Follette Hearings,* pt. 25, 10809, 10813.

76. Quoted in "Fink Racket: Report on Strike-breaking Prepared by the La Follette Civil Liberties Committee," *Nation,* Feb. 11, 1939, 165.

77. National Labor Relations Board, *First Annual Report of the National Labor Relations Board,* 75, 73.

78. *Hearings on S. 1970,* 131.

79. Ibid., 130–31.

80. Ibid.

81. *Industrial Espionage,* 67.

82. Ibid.

83. *La Follette Hearings,* pt. 1, 205.

84. *Industrial Espionage,* 66, quoted in Huberman, *Labor Spy Racket,* 30–31.

85. *Hearings on S. 1970,* 182.

86. *Hearings on 266,* 302.

87. *Strikebreaking Services,* 114.

88. *Hearings on 266,* 295.

89. Patrick J. Maney, *"Young Bob" La Follette: A Biography of Robert M. La Follette Jr., 1895–1953* (Columbia: University of Missouri Press, 1978), 170; American Federation of Labor, *Proceedings of the Fifty-Fifth Annual Convention* (1935), 610.

90. Gilbert J. Gall, "Heber Blankenhorn, the La Follette Committee, and the Irony of Industrial Repression," *Labor History* 23 (spring 1982): 246–47.

91. *Congressional Record,* 74th Congress, 2nd Session (1936), 80: 41

92. *Hearings on 266,* 2–3.

93. Jerold S. Auerbach, *Labor and Liberty: The La Follette Committee and the New Deal* (New York: Bobbs-Merrill and Company, 1966), 71–73.

94. Dwight McDonald, "Espionage Inc.," *Nation,* Feb. 27, 1937, 239; Blankenhorn to J. Warren Madden, Dec. 19, 1936, quoted in Maney, *"Young Bob" La Follette,* 174.

95. *Strikebreaking Services,* 19.

96. *New York Times,* 13 August 1936, 1; *New York Times,* February 9, 1937, 7.

97. *La Follettte Hearings*, pt. 5, 1706.

98. Quoted in E. T. Buehrer, "Big Business Sows the Wind," *Christian Century*, Mar. 16, 1938, 330.

99. *La Follette Hearings*, pt. 1, 16.

100. *Hearings on S. 1970*, 12.

101. Quoted in "Spy Profits," *Literary Digest*, Mar. 27, 1937, 5.

102. "To Make Employers Fight Fair: Oppressive Labor Practices Act of 1939," *New Republic*, May 3, 1939, 365.

103. *Congressional Record*, 76th Congress, 1st Session, 1939, 84:4864–65.

104. *Hearings on S. 1970*, 169.

105. *New York Times*, May, 24, 1940, 9.

106. *Congressional Record*, 76th Congress, 3rd Session, 1940, 86:6693, 6707.

107. Ibid., 6904–6.

108. *Time*, June 10, 1940, 19.

109. Quoted in James D. Horan, *The Pinkertons: The Detective Dynasty that Made History* (New York: Crown Publishers, 1967), 509.

110. Ibid.

111. Ibid., 510.

112. D. S., "Industrial Spying in Trade Unions," *Workers Age*, Jan. 1938, 8.

113. *Hearings on S. 1970*, 138.

114. Ibid., 143.

115. Ibid., 201.

Chapter Four

1. To better understand the postwar struggle between business and organized labor see Elizabeth A. Fones-Wolf, *Selling Free Enterprise: The Business Assault on Labor and Liberalism. 1945–1960* (Urbana: University of Illinois Press, 1994).

2. *New York Times*, Feb. 5, 1968, 35; Nathan W. Shefferman, with Dale Kramer, *The Man in the Middle* (Garden City, N.Y.: Doubleday and Company, 1961), 9–10.

3. U.S. Congress, Senate, *Interim Report of the Select Committee on Improper Activities in the Labor or Management Field*, 86th Congress, 2nd Session, S. Report No. 1417 (1958), 255 (hereafter cited as *Interim Report*); "Now Employers Are Under Fire," *U.S. News and World Report*, Nov.1, 1957, 95.

4. *Interim Report*, 298, 255.

5. Daniel Bell, "Nate Shefferman Union Buster," *Fortune*, Feb. 1958, 120–21, 204–5.

6. *Interim Report*, 255–56; Bureau of National Affairs, *The McClellan Committee Hearings, 1957* (Washington, D.C.: Bureau of National Affairs, 1958), 333.

7. Bureau of National Affairs, *McClellan Committee Hearings, 1957*, 334.

8. "For Labor, For Management, For Shefferman," *Newsweek*, Nov. 4, 1957, 33; Bell, "Nate Shefferman Union Buster," 120–21.

9. "Now Employers Are Under Fire," 98.

10. *Interim Report*, 258–60.

11. Ibid.

12. U.S. Congress, Senate, Committee on Education and Labor, *Investigation of Improper Activities in Labor or Management Field*, Hearings, 85th Congress, 1st Session (Washington, D.C.: Government Printing Office, 1957), pt. 15, 5779–84, 5984 (hereafter cited as *Investigation of Improper Activities*); *Interim Report*, 259–69, 265–66; *Investigation of Improper Activities*, pt. 15, 5781.

13. *Interim Report*, 256.

14. Bell, "Nate Shefferman Union Buster," 120.

15. *Interim Report*, 298; John Hutchinson, *The Imperfect Union: A History of Corruption in American Trade Unions* (New York: E. P. Dutton and Company, 1972), 181–82.

16. This committee consisted of four Democrats (McClellan of Arkansas, Sam J. Ervin of North Carolina, Robert F. Kennedy of Massachusetts, and Patrick V. McNamara of Michigan) and an equal number of Republicans (Irving Ives of New York, Eugene McCarthy of Wisconsin, Karl E. Mundt of South Dakota, and Barry Goldwater of Arizona).

17. More than 70 percent of Shefferman's forty most important clients utilized his services to battle unionization drives, committee members discovered.

18. Bell, "Nate Shefferman Union Buster," 121.

19. Quoted in Hutchinson, *Imperfect Union*, 181–82.

20. "Employers' Turn on the Stand," *Business Week*, Nov. 9, 1957, 32.

21. U.S. Congress, Senate, *Labor-Management Disclosure Act of 1959*, 86th Congress, 1st Session, S. Report 187, 6.

22. *Interim Report*, 300.

23. U.S. Congress, House of Representatives, Report of the Subcommittee on Labor Management Relations of the Committee on Education and Labor, *The Forgotten Law: Disclosure of Consultant and Employer Activity Under the L.M.R.D.A.*, 98th Congress, 2nd Session (1985), 3 (hereafter cited as *Report on Oversight Hearings*).

24. Indeed, one finds little evidence of these agencies during the early 1960s.

25. Shefferman and Kramer, *The Man in the Middle*; *New York Times*, Feb. 5, 1968, 35.

26. Quoted in John L. McClellan, *Crime Without Punishment* (New York: Duell, Sloan and Pearce, 1962), 203; address given by Robert P. Griffin, Labor Law Section of the Michigan State Bar, Annual Meeting, Sept. 25, 1959.

27. U.S. Congress, House of Representatives, Committee on Education and Labor, Report of the Subcommittee on Labor-Management Relations, *Pressures in Today's Workplace*, 96th Congress, 2nd Session (1980), 38 (hereafter cited as *Report on Pressures in Today's Workplace*). U.S. Department of Labor, Office of Labor-Management Standards Enforcement, Labor Management Services Administration, "Compliance, Enforcement and Reporting," 25. See also *Report on Pressures in Today's Workplace*, 44.

28. U.S. Department of Labor, Office of Labor-Management Standards Enforcement, Labor-Management Services Administration, "Labor-Management Services Administration Message" No. 19–80, Mar. 6, 1980.

29. The Bureau of National Affairs, *Labor Relations Consultants: Issues, Trends and Controversies*, A Bureau of National Affairs Special Report (Washington, D.C.: Bureau of National Affairs, 1985), 31.

30. U.S. Congress, House of Representatives, Subcommittee on Labor Management

Relations of the Committee on Education and Labor, 96th Congress, 1st Session, *Pressure in Today's Workplace,* vol. 4, 2 (hereafter cited as *Pressures Hearings*).

31. *Pressures Hearings,* vol. 3, 112.

32. Ibid., vol. 3, 313, 422–23.

33. National Labor Relations Board, *Forty-fifth Annual Report of the National Labor Relations Board* (Washington, D.C.: Government Printing Office, 1980), 269–73.

34. Ibid.

35. *Pressures Hearings,* vol. 3, 124–25.

36. Quoted in Steve Lagerfield, "To Break a Union," *Harper's,* May 1981, 16.

37. Quoted in Bureau of National Affairs, *Labor Relations Consultants,* 12.

38. Letter to Diana Mulvihill, of Record Data, Inc., of New York, Jan. 27, 1984, reprinted in New York State Legislature, "A Report on the Plight of the Collective Bargaining System," Jan. 1984, 35.

39. *Report on Pressures in Today's Workplace,* 28.

40. "Firms Learn Art of Keeping Unions Out," *Wall Street Journal,* Apr. 19, 1977, 48.

41. Ibid.

42. *AMR Reporter: Trends and Strategies in Maintaining Non-Union Status,* Mar. 1980.

43. New York State Legislature, Standing Committee on Labor, "Report on the Misuse of Medicaid Funds to Deprive Workers of their Right to Join a Union," Mar. 1982, 11.

44. "Firms Learn Art of Keeping Unions Out," 48.

45. Ibid.

46. *Pressures Hearings,* vol. 1, 27.

47. Transcript of tape recording made from a September 1980 seminar entitled "Update: Labor Relations," sponsored by the New Jersey Association of Health Care Facilities, New York State Legislature, Standing Committee on Labor, "Report on the Misuse of Medicaid Funds to Deprive Workers of their Right to Join a Union," Mar. 1982, exhibit A, 17–19.

48. Alfred DeMaria, *How Management Wins Union Organizing Campaigns* (New York: Executive Enterprises Publications 1980), 121.

49. Transcript of seminar quoted in *Pressures Hearings,* vol. 1, 196–98.

50. New York State Legislature, Standing Committee on Labor, "Report on the Misuse of Medicaid Funds to Deprive Workers of their Right to Join a Union," Mar. 1982, 45.

51. *Report on Pressures in Today's Workplace,* 39.

52. Pamphlet published by Human Resources and Profits Associates, Inc., reprinted in New York State Legislature "Report on the Plight," 38; Executive Enterprises, Inc., "The Process of De certification," pamphlet reprinted in *Pressures Hearings,* vol. 1, 51–52.

53. Quoted in Center to Protect Workers' Rights, *From Brass Knuckles to Briefcases: The Changing Art of Union Busting in America* (Washington, D.C.: Center to Protect Workers' Rights, 1979), 41.

54. William E. Fulmer, "When Employees Want to Oust their Union," *Harvard Business Review* 56 (Mar.–Apr. 1978); National Labor Relations Board, *Thirty-third Annual Report of the National Labor Relations Board* (Washington, D.C.: Government Printing Office, 1967), 10; National Labor Relations Board, *Forty-second Annual Report of the National Labor Relations Board* (Washington, D.C.: Government Printing Office, 1977), 296.

55. National Labor Relations Board, *Decisions and Orders of the National Labor Relations Board*, vol. 263 (1982), 834, 847–48.

56. *Pressures Hearings*, vol. 3, 76.

57. Ibid., 213.

58. Pamphlet prepared by West Coast Industrial Relations Associates, "The Non-Union Company," 45, reprinted in *Pressures Hearings*, vol. 1, 278.

59. National Labor Relations Board, *Decisions and Orders of the National Labor Relations Board*, vol. 204 (1973), 921, 926–27.

60. *Report on Pressures in Today's Work Place*, 33.

61. DeMaria, *How Management Wins Union Organizing Campaigns*, 192.

62. *Pressures Hearings*, vol. 1, 212–14.

63. West Coast Industrial Relations Associates, "The Non-Union Company," 45, reprinted in *Pressures Hearings*, vol. 1, 278.

64. National Labor Relations Board, *Decisions and Orders of the National Labor Relations Board*, vol. 263, (1982), 834–44.

65. *Report on Pressures in Today's Workplace*, 35.

66. Letter dated May 16, 1980, reprinted in New York State Legislature, Standing Committee on Labor, "Report on the Misuse of Medicaid Funds to Deprive Workers of their Right to Join a Union," Mar. 1982, appendix B.

67. Martin J. Levitt, with Terry Conrow, *Confessions of a Union Buster* (New York: Crown Publishers, 1983), 194.

68. National Labor Relations Board, *Decisions and Orders of the National Labor Relations Board*, vol. 199 (1972), 250–61.

69. Levitt, *Confessions of a Union Buster*, 13.

70. *Pressures Hearings*, vol. 1, 196.

71. National Labor Relations Board, *International Union of Electrical Workers v. NLRB*, 426 F.2d, 1243 (D.C. cir.) 400 U.S. 950 (1970).

72. National Labor Relations Board, *Decisions and Orders of the National Labor Relations Board*, vol. 205 (1973), 512–15.

73. Transcript of tape recording made from the Sept. 27, 1974, seminar entitled "Update: Labor Relations," sponsored by the New Jersey Associations of Health Care Facilities, New York State Legislature, Standing Committee on Labor, "Report on the Misuse of Medicaid Funds to Deprive Workers of their Right to Join a Union," Mar. 1982, exhibit A.

74. National Labor Relations Board, *Decisions and Orders of the National Labor Relations Board*, vol. 245 (1979), 1347–52.

75. *Pressures Hearings*, vol. 1, 112.

76. *Report on Pressures in Today's Workplace*, 36

77. Ibid., 51, 1–2.

78. Ibid., 1–2, 25, 38.

79. *Pressures Hearings*, vol. 1, 85–86.

80. *Report on Pressures in Today's Workplace*, 45–47.

81. Ibid., 47; *Pressures Hearings*, vol. 4, 242, 7; *Report on Oversight Hearings*, 331.

82. "Consultants checklist," *R.U.B. Sheet,* Sept. 8, 1979, 1–2.

83. AFL-CIO, *Report of the Executive Council of the AFL-CIO: Thirteenth Convention,* 1979, 121–26; "Labor Fights Back Against Union Busters," *U.S. News and World Report,* Dec. 10, 1979, 98.

84. AFL-CIO, *Report of the Executive Council of the AFL-CIO: Fifteenth Convention,* Oct. 3, 1983, 120; Joanne Lublin, "Labor Strikes Back at Consultants that Help Firms Keep Unions Out," *Wall Street Journal,* Apr. 2, 1981, 29.

85. Lublin, "Labor Strikes Back at Consultants that Help Firms Keep Unions Out," 29.

86. *Report on Oversight Hearings,* 367.

87. Ibid., 9.

88. U.S. Congress, House, Subcommittee on Labor-Management Relations, Staff of House Committee on Education and Labor, 98th Congress, 2nd Session, *Report Concerning Enforcement of Consultant and Employer Reporting Provisions of the Landrum-Griffin Act* (Committee Print, 1984), 9; *Report on Oversight Hearings,* 313.

89. Robert H. Zieger, *American Workers, American Unions,* 1920–1985 (Baltimore: Johns Hopkins University Press), 192, 199.

Epilogue

1. John Hoerr, "A Host of Strikebreakers Is Tipping the Scales Against Labor," *Business Week,* July 15, 1985, 32.

2. Peter T. Kilborn, "California Strike Becomes a Battle over Permanent Job Replacements," *New York Times,* Apr. 17, 1994, 22.

3. "Struggle over Striker Replacements," *Baltimore Sun,* Mar. 16, 1995, 16A; David Bacon, "Labor Slaps the Smug New Face of Union-Busting," *Covert Action Quarterly* 31 (spring 1997): 4.

4. Kevin Kelly, "Picket Lines? Just Call 1–800 Strikebreaker," *Business Week,* Mar. 27, 1995, 42.

5. Bacon, "Labor Slaps the Smug New Face of Union-Busting," 4; Kelly, "Picket Lines?" 42.

6. Josh Daniel, "Sisters, Can You Spare a Dime?" *Nation,* July 10, 1995, 55.

7. Bacon, "Labor Slaps the Smug New Face of Union-Busting," 4.

8. Ibid.; Raja Mishra, "To Serve and Protect—For a Price," *Detroit Journal,* Aug. 4, 1995, 1.

9. Frank Swoboda, "On a Mission to Find Security in the Protection Business" *Washington Post,* May 26, 1996, F11; Mike Ashley, "Keeping an Eye on Profits," *Virginia Business,* May 1, 1998, 1.

10. Kim Isaac Eisler, "Secret Service Inc.," *Washingtonian* 31 (May 1996): 48–49; Ashley, "Keeping an Eye on Profits," 1.

11. Ashley, "Keeping an Eye on Profits," 1.

12. Vance International homepage (<http://www.vancesecurity.com/index.htm>).

13. Ashley, "Keeping an Eye on Profits," 1.

14. James L. Pate, "Guerrilla War in the Hills: Mercs Come to Appalachia," *Soldier of Fortune,* Sept. 1986, 67.

15. Quoted in Pate, "Guerrilla War in the Hills," 67, 69, 94.

16. James R. Green, "Tying the Knot of Solidarity: The Pittston Strike of 1989–1990," in *The United Mine Workers of America: A Model of Industrial Solidarity,* ed. John M. Laslett (University Park: Pennsylvania State University Press, 1996), 519.

17. Dwayne Yancy, "Thunder in The Coal Fields: The UMW's Strike Against Pittston," *Roanoke Times and World News,* Apr. 29, 1990, 8.

18. Quoted in a Vance pamphlet in author's possession.

19. *Louisville Courier Journal,* June 28, 1989, 3B; Labor in America, *"We Won't Go Back": UMWA/Pittston Strike, 1989–90* (Clinchco, Va.: Dickenson Star, 1990), 41.

20. *Louisville Courier Journal,* June 28, 1989, 3B; Yancy, "Thunder in The Coal Fields," 4.

21. *Los Angeles Times,* June 24, 1989, pt. 1, 1.

22. Charles F. Vance, "Picture-Perfect Strike Protection," *Security Management* 35, no. 11 (Nov. 1991): 47.

23. Virginia St. Paul, "Christians and the Coalfield Conflict," *Christian Century,* Oct. 4, 1989, 869.

24. Vance, "Picture-Perfect Strike Protection," 47.

25. Ashley, "Keeping an Eye on Profits," 1.

26. Patrick H. McHaffie, "The Spatialization of Union Busting: The Pittston Strike," unpublished paper in author's possession, 23.

27. Michael deCourcy Hinds, "Bitter Coal Strike May Be at End," *New York Times,* Dec. 23, 1989, 17.

28. *Detroit Sunday Journal,* Mar. 9, 1997, 10. Letters submitted to the Michigan State House of Representatives, Labor and Occupational Committee as well as committee notes listing witnesses and what they were scheduled to testify about are in author's possession. These hearings were not recorded.

29. Michigan State House of Representatives document in author's possession.

30. UPI, Mar. 21, 1990, BC cycle.

31. "What Should We Do?" *Ammo* 30, no. 1 (Jan. 1998) (<www.uaw.org/ammo_mag/ammo3001/10.html>).

32. "McDonnell Workers File Charges with NLRB," UPI, July 3, 1996, BC cycle.

33. Alexander Cockburn, "Clinton Speech Leaves Labor Hanging," *Star Tribune,* Oct. 15, 1993, 23A; Frank Swoboda and Helen Dewar, "Labor Makes Startling Offer to Congress," *Los Angeles Times,* June 11, 1992, D4.

34. Jack Torry, "Reich Wants to Ban Hiring Striker Replacements," *Pittsburgh Post-Gazette,* Mar. 31, 1993, B12.

35. "After the Strike," *New York Times,* Feb. 23, 1995, A22.

36. Martin Kasindorf, "Exec. Order Bars Hiring Replacements," *Newsday,* Mar. 9, 1995, A17.

37. "Clinton Ban Expected Today on Replacement of Strikers," *Atlanta Journal-Constitution,* Mar. 8, 1995, 5D; Tim Shorrock, "Steel Workers Reach Pact," *Journal of Commerce,* Nov. 6, 1996, 5A; Kelly, "Picket Lines?" 42.

38. Kasindorf, "Exec. Order Bars Hiring Replacements," A17.

39. Bob Drummond, "Clinton Strike Policy Upheld," *Chicago Sun-Times,* Aug. 1, 1995, 46.

40. <http://www.vancesecurity.com/frames/main5>; Grant Sesek, "Asarco: Strike Guards Working without Licenses," Helena (Montana) *Independent Record,* Feb. 24, 1999.

41. Tom Johnson, "Caterpillar Bulldozes the United Auto Workers," *Business and Society Review* 96 (1996): 39.

42. Randolph Heaster, "Strikers Walk; Security Watches," *Kansas City Star,* June 6, 1997, B1.

43. Mike Zielinski, "Armed and Dangerous: Private Police on the March," *Covert Action Quarterly* (<http://mediafilter.org/caq/CAQ54p.police.html>).

44. (<http://specialprotection.com/strikeguide.htm>).

45. (<http://www.specialresponse.com/>); Robert Sherefkin, "JCI Beefs Up Security at Taylor Plant," *Crain's Detroit Business,* Feb. 10, 1997, 1.

46. Doug Grow, "Behemoth Pepsi Short on Gratitude," *Star Tribune,* Aug. 20, 2000, 2B.

47. Diana E. Lewis, "Temporary Nursing Agency Gives Massachusetts Hospitals Options amid Strikes," *Boston Globe,* Apr. 6, 2000.

BIBLIOGRAPHY

Manuscript Collections

The American Federation of Labor Records, the Samuel Gompers Papers, McKeldin Library, University of Maryland, College Park, Maryland

Elias M. Ammons Papers, Division of State Archives, Denver, Colorado

The Hawley and William E. Borah Manuscripts, Idaho Historical Society, Boise

Commission on Industrial Relations, 1912–1915 collection, State Historical Society of Wisconsin, Madison

Papers of Governor George Hoadly, 1884–86, MS Collection #314, Ohio Historical Society, Columbus

Joseph Labadie Collection, University of Michigan Graduate Library, Ann Arbor

Allan Pinkerton Papers, Library of Congress, Washington, D.C.

World Wide Web

(Note: World Wide Web sites are accurate as of the time of publication.)

<http://specialprotection.com/strikeguide.htm>

<http://www.specialresponse.com/>

The Labor Films Guide (<http://www.nathannewman.org.EDIN/.labor/.resource/.films.html>).

Vance International homepage (<http://www.vancesecurity.com/index.htm>).

"What Should We Do?" *Ammo* 30, no. 1 (Jan. 1998), <www.uaw.org/ammo_mag/ammo3001/10.html>.

Zielinski, Mike. "Armed and Dangerous: Private Police on the March" *Covert Action Quarterly* (<http://mediafilter.org/caq/CAQ54p.police.html>).

Bibliography

Government Documents

Bureau of National Affairs. *The McClellan Committee Hearings, 1957* (Washington, D.C.: Bureau of National Affairs, 1958).

———. *Labor Relations Consultants: Issues, Trends and Controversies,* A Bureau of National Affairs Special Report (Washington, D.C.: Bureau of National Affairs, 1985).

Colorado Adjunct General's Office. *The Military Occupation of the Coal Strike Zone of Colorado, by the Colorado National Guard, 1913–14: Report of the Commanding General to the Governor, Colorado, 1914* (Denver: Press of the Smith-Brooks Printing Company, 1914).

Committee on Coal and Civil Liberties. "Coal and Civil Liberties, Report to the U.S. Coal Commission" (report submitted Aug. 11, 1923), U.S. Department of Labor Library, Washington, D.C., 14–20.

Commonwealth of Massachussetts. *Proceedings of the Twenty-sixth Annual Convention of the Massachusetts State Board of the AFL* (1911).

Commonwealth of Pennsylvania. *Laws of the Commonwealth of Pennsylvania Passed in the Session of 1893* (Harrisburg: E. K. Meyers, State Printer, 1893).

National Labor Relations Board. *Decisions and Orders of the National Labor Relations Board,* vol. 2 (Washington, D.C.: Government Printing Office, 1937).

———. *First Annual Report* (Washington, D.C.: Government Printing Office, 1937).

———. *Decisions and Orders of the National Labor Relations Board,* vol. 8 (Washington, D.C.: Government Printing Office, 1938), 447.

———. *Decisions and Orders of the National Labor Relations Board,* vol. 9 (Washington, D.C.: Government Printing Office, 1938), 546.

———. *Thirty-third Annual Report of the National Labor Relations Board* (Washington, D.C.: Government Printing Office, 1967).

———. *International Union of Electrical Workers v. NLRB,* 426 F.2d, 1243 (D.C. cir.) 400, U.S. 950 (1970).

———. *Decisions and Orders of the National Labor Relations Board,* vol. 199 (Washington, D.C.: Government Printing Office, 1972), 250–61.

———. *Decisions and Orders of the National Labor Relations Board,* vol. 204 (Washington, D.C.: Government Printing Office, 1973), 921, 926–27.

———. *Decisions and Orders of the National Labor Relations Board,* vol. 205 (Washington, D.C.: Government Printing Office, 1973), 512–15.

———. *Forty-second Annual Report of the National Labor Relations Board* (Washington, D.C.: Government Printing Office, 1977).

———. *Decisions and Orders of the National Labor Relations Board,* vol. 245 (Washington, D.C.: Government Printing Office, 1979), 1347–52.

————. *Forty-fifth Annual Report of the National Labor Relations Board* (Washington, D.C.: Government Printing Office, 1980).

————. *Decisions and Orders of the National Labor Relations Board,* vol. 263 (Washington, D.C.: Government Printing Office, 1982), 834–44, 847–48.

New York State Legislature, Standing Committee on Labor. Charles F. Peck, *Fifth Annual Report of the Bureau of Statistics of Labor for the Year 1887,* Assembly Document No. 47, Albany, 1888.

————. "Update: Labor Relations." Transcript of tape recording made from a September 1980 seminar sponsored by the New Jersey Association of Health Care Facilities.

————. "Report on the Misuse of Medicaid Funds to Deprive Workers of their Right to Join a Union," Mar. 1982.

————. "A Report on the Plight of the Collective Bargaining System," pamphlet published by Human Resources and Profits Associates, Inc., reprinted in Standing Committee on Labor, New York State Assembly, Jan. 1984.

State of Illinois. *Journal of the House of Representatives of the Thirty-Sixth General Assembly of the State of Illinois.* (Springfield, Ill.: State Printing Office, 1889).

————. *Journal of the House of Representatives of the Thirty-eighth General Assembly of the State of Illinois.* (Springfield, Ill.: State Printing Office, 1893).

————. *Laws of 1893,* 129.

State of Louisiana. Report of the Bureau of Statistics of Labor for the State of Louisiana, 1902–3.

State of New Jersey. Annual Report of the New Jersey Bureau of Statistics of Labor and Industries, Trenton, 1916.

State of West Virginia. Report of the West Virginia Mining Commission, appointed by Governor William E. Glasscock on the 28th Day of August 1912 (Charleston: n.p., 1912).

U.S. Coal Commission. *Report of the United States Coal Commission* (Washington, D.C.: Government Printing Office, 1923).

————. *Report of the United States Coal Commission,* pt. 1 (Washington, D.C.: Government Printing Office, 1925).

U.S. Commission on Industrial Relations. *First Annual Report of the Commission on Industrial Relations* (Washington, D.C.: Barnard and Miller, 1914).

————. *Final Report of the Commission on Industrial Relations* (Washington, D.C.: Barnard and Miller, 1915).

————. George P. West, *Report on the Colorado Strike* (Washington, D.C.: s.n., 1915).

————. *Final Report and Testimony of the Commission on Industrial Relations* (Washington, D.C.: Government Printing Office, 1916), 7:6439.

U.S. Congress. House of Representatives, 52nd Congress, 1st Session, House Report #2447, 1892, "Investigation of the Employment of Pinkerton Men."

————. *Congressional Record,* 52nd Congress, 1st Session, 1893, 23: 4223, 4225, pt. 5.

————. Senate, 52nd Congress, 2nd Session, Senate Report no. 1280, "Investigation of Labor Troubles at Homestead," 1893.

————. House of Representatives, *Peonage in Western Pennsylvania,* Hearings before the Committee on Labor of the House of Representatives, 62nd Congress, 1st Session, Aug. 1, 1911 (Washington, D.C.: Government Printing Office, 1911).

————. Senate, Committee on Education and Labor, *Conditions in the Paint Creek District West Virginia,* Hearings pursuant to Senate Resolution no. 37, 63rd Congress, 1st Session, 1913 (Washington, D.C.: Government Printing Office, 1913).

————. Senate, 63rd Congress, 2nd Session, Senate Document no. 381, *Report on the Strike in the Copper Mining District of Michigan,* 1914, 59.

————. House of Representatives, 63rd Congress, 3rd Session, House Document no. 1630, *Report on the Colorado Strike Investigation* (Washington, D.C.: Government Printing Office, 1915).

————. Senate, *Final Report and Testimony of The United States Commission of Industrial Relations,* II. S. Doc. no. 415, 64th Congress, 1st Session, 1916.

————. Senate, Committee on Education and Labor, Hearings pursuant to Senate Resolution no. 80, to Investigate Recent Acts of Violence in the Coal Fields of West Virginia, 67th Congress, 1st Session, 1921–22. Vols. 1, 2.

————. House of Representatives, 74th Congress, 2nd Session, House Report no. 2431, 1935.

————. Senate, 74th Congress, 2nd Session, Senate Report no. 1420, 1935.

————. *Congressional Record,* 74th Congress, 2nd Session, 1936, 80.

————. Senate, Committee on Education and Labor, 74th Congress, 2nd Session, *Hearings on 266* (Washington, D.C.: Government Printing Office, 1936).

————. Senate, Subcommittee of the Committee on Education and Labor, Hearings pursuant to Senate Resolution no. 266, *Violations of Free Speech and Rights of Labor,* 74th–76th Congress, 1936–39.

————. Senate, Committee on Education and Labor, *Industrial Espionage,* Senate Report no. 46, pt. 3, 75th Congress, 2nd Session, 1937.

————. *Congressional Record,* 76th Congress, 1st Session, 1939.

————. Senate, Committee on Education and Labor, *Hearings on Senate Bill 1970,* 76th Congress, 1st Session, 1939.

————. Senate, Committee on Education and Labor, *Labor Policies of Employer's Associations, The National Association of Manufacturers,* Senate Report no. 6, pt. 6, 76th Congress, 1st Session, 1939.

————. Senate, Committee on Education and Labor, *Private Police Systems,* Senate Report 6, pt. 2, 76th Congress, 1st Session, 1939.

———. Senate, Subcommittee of the Committee on Education and Labor, *Strike-breaking Services*, S. Report 6, pt. 1, 76th Congress, 1st Session, 1939.

———. *Congressional Record*, 76th Congress, 3rd Session, 1940.

———. Senate, Committee on Education and Labor, *Investigation of Improper Activities in Labor or Management Field*, Hearings, 85th Congress, 1st Session (Washington, D.C.: Government Printing Office, 1957).

———. Senate, *Labor-Management Disclosure Act of 1959*, 86th Congress, 1st Session, Senate Report no. 187, 6.

———. Senate, *Interim Report of the Select Committee on Improper Activities in the Labor or Management Field*, 86th Congress, 2nd Session, Senate Report no. 1417, 1958.

———. House of Representatives, Subcommittee on Labor-Management Relations of the Committee on Education and Labor, 96th Congress, 1st Session, *Pressure in Today's Workplace*, 1979.

———. House of Representatives, Committee on Education and Labor, Report of the Subcommittee on Labor-Management Relations, *Pressures in Today's Workplace*, 96th Congress, 2nd Session, 1980.

———. House of Representatives, Subcommittee on Labor-Management Relations, Staff of the House Committee on Education and Labor, 98th Congress, 2nd Session, *Report Concerning Enforcement of Consultant and Employer Reporting Provisions of the Landrum-Griffin Act*, Committee Print, 1984.

———. House of Representatives, Report of the Subcommittee on Labor-Management Relations of the Committee on Education and Labor, *The Forgotten Law: Disclosure of Consultant and Employer Activity Under the L.M.R.D.A.*, 98th Congress, 2nd Session, 1985.

U.S. Department of Labor, Office of Labor-Management Services Administration, "News Bulletin to Professionals," no. 80–82, Feb. 1980, "Summary of Employer and Consultant Reporting Cases."

———. Office of Labor-Management Standards Enforcement, Labor-Management Services Administration, "Compliance, Enforcement and Reporting."

———. Office of Labor-Management Standards Enforcement, Labor-Management Services Administration, "Labor-Management Services Administration Message" no. 19–80, Mar. 6, 1980.

U.S. Industrial Commission on Labor Legislation. *Sixteenth Annual Report of the Commissioner of Labor*, vol. 16 (Washington, D.C.: Government Printing Office, 1901), 992–1033.

———. *Final Report of the Industrial Commission*, vol. 19 (Washington, D.C.: Government Printing Office, 1902).

West Virginia Legislature, *Acts*, 1913, 173–74.

Theses and Dissertations

Ensley, Philip C. "The Interchurch World Movement and the Steel Strike of 1919." M.A. thesis, Ohio State University, 1962.

Hogg, Bernard J. "The Homestead Strike of 1892." Ph.D. diss., University of Chicago, 1943.

Lozier, John William. "The Hocking Valley Coal Miners' Strike, 1884–1885." M.A. thesis, Ohio State University, 1936.

McHaffie, Patrick H. "The Spatialization of Union Busting: The Pittston Strike." Unpublished paper in author's possession.

Myers, Howard B. "The Policing of Labor Disputes in Chicago." Ph.D. diss., University of Chicago, 1929.

Rappaport, Leonard. "The United States Commission on Industrial Relations." M.A. thesis, George Washington University, 1957.

Roberts, Thomas. "A History and Analysis of Labor-Management Relations in the Philadelphia Transit Industry." Ph.D. diss., University of Pennsylvania, 1959.

Waitzman, Samuel. "The New York Transit Strike of 1916." M.A. thesis, Columbia University, 1952.

Publications

Adams, Graham Jr. *Age of Industrial Violence, The Activities and Findings of the United States Commission on Industrial Relations,* 1910–15 (New York: Columbia University Press, 1966).

AFL-CIO. *Report of the Executive Council of the AFL-CIO: Thirteenth Convention,* 1979, 121–26.

———. *Report of the Executive Council of the AFL-CIO: Fifteenth Convention,* Oct. 3, 1983.

"After the Strike." *New York Times,* Feb. 23, 1995, A22.

American Federation of Labor. *Proceedings of the Fifty-Fifth Annual Convention,* 1935.

American Industries (Apr. 1905): 3.

———. (May 1906): inside cover.

Amidon, Beulah. "Employers and the Spy Business." *Survey Graphic,* May 1937, 266.

AMR Reporter: Trends and Strategies in Maintaining Non-Union Status, Mar. 1980.

Ashley, Mike. "Keeping an Eye on Profits." *Virginia Business,* May 1, 1998, 1.

Auerbach, Jerold S. *Labor and Liberty: The La Follette Committee and the New Deal* (New York: Bobbs-Merrill and Company, 1966).

Avrich, Paul. *The Haymarket Tragedy* (Princeton, N.J.: Princeton University Press, 1984).

Bacon, David. "Labor Slaps the Smug New Face of Union-Busting." *Covert Action Quarterly* 31 (spring 1997).

Baily, Kenneth R. "Grim Visaged Men and the West Virginia National Guard in the 1912–1913 Paint and Cabin Creek Strike." *West Virginia History* 41, no. 2 (winter 1986).

Basso, Hamilton. "Strike-Buster: Man Among Men." *New Republic*, Dec. 12, 1934, 125.

Bean, Walton. *Boss Ruef's San Francisco: The Story of the Union Labor Party, Big Business, and the Graft Prosecution* (Berkeley: University of California Press, 1967).

Beet, Thomas. "Methods of Private Detective Agencies." *Appleton's Magazine*, Oct. 1906, 445.

Bell, Daniel. "Nate Shefferman Union Buster." *Fortune*, Feb. 1958, 120–21, 204–5.

Bernstein, Irving. *The Lean Years: A History of the American Worker, 1919–1929* (Boston: Houghton, Mifflin Company, 1960).

———. *The Turbulent Years: A History of the American Worker* (Boston: Houghton, Mifflin Company, 1970).

Birtles, Andrew. "Governor George Hoadly's Use of the Ohio National Guard in the Hocking Valley Coal Strike of 1884." *Ohio History* 91 (1982).

Bogart, Ernest L. *The Centennial History of Chicago: The Industrial State, 1870–1893*, vol. 4 (Chicago: A. C. McClurg and Company, 1922).

Brent, Henry K. "The Strike Situation in San Francisco." *Street Railway Journal* 30, no. 12 (Sept. 21, 1907): 417–18.

Brody, David. *Steel Workers in America: The Nonunion Era* (New York: Harper and Row Publishers, 1960).

Brooks, Robert B. B. *When Labor Organizes* (New Haven: Yale University Press, 1938).

Buehrer, E. T. "Big Business Sows the Wind." *Christian Century*, Mar. 16, 1938, 330.

Buhle, Paul, Scott Molloy, and Gail Sansbury, eds. *A History of Rhode Island Working People* (Providence: Regine Printing Company, 1983).

Carmen, Harry J., Henry David, and Paul N. Guthrie, eds. *The Path I Trod: The Autobiography of Terrence V. Powderly* (New York: Columbia University Press, 1940).

Caulkins, Clinch. *Spy Overhead: The Story of Industrial Espionage* (New York: Harcourt, Brace and Company, 1937).

Center to Protect Workers' Rights. *From Brass Knuckles to Briefcases: The Changing Art of Union Busting in America* (Washington, D.C.: Center to Protect Workers' Rights, 1979).

Chaplin, Ralph. *When the Leaves Come Out and Other Rebel Verses* (Cleveland: author, 1917).

Christian, W. Asbury. *Richmond: Her Past and Present* (Richmond: L. H. Jenkins, 1912).

"Clinton Ban Expected Today on Replacement of Strikers." *Atlanta Journal-Constitution*, Mar. 8, 1995, 5D.

Cockburn, Alexander. "Clinton Speech Leaves Labor Hanging." *Star Tribune*, Oct. 15, 1993, 23A.

Commons, John R. *Myself* (Madison: University of Wisconsin Press, 1964).

Conley, Phil M. *Life in a West Virginia Coal Field* (Charleston: American Constitutional Association, 1923).

Conner, Valerie Jean. *The National War Labor Board* (Chapel Hill: University of North Carolina Press, 1983).

"Consultants Checklist." *R.U.B. Sheet*, Sept. 8, 1979, 1–2.

Cook, Bob. "Schools Tap Security Force in Case of Strike." *Crain's Cleveland Business*, Sept. 16, 1996, 3.

Corbin, David Alan. *Life, Work, and Rebellion in the Coal Fields: The Southern West Virginia Miners, 1880–1922* (Urbana: University of Illinois Press, 1981).

Cox, Harold. "The Wilkes-Barre Street Railway Strike of 1915." *Pennsylvania Magazine of History and Biography* 94 (1970).

Cronin, James E., and Carmen Siriann, eds. *Work, Community, and Power* (Philadelphia: Temple University Press, 1983).

Crowe, Kenneth. "Top Teamsters." *Newsday*, Feb. 28, 1993, 92

"The Culprits Cry 'Stop Thief!'" *American Federationist*, Jan. 1904, 35.

Daniel, Josh. "Sisters, Can You Spare a Dime?" *Nation*, July 10, 1995, 55.

DeBrizzi, John A. "The Standard Oil Strikes in Bayonne, New Jersey, 1915–16." *New Jersey History* 101 (1983).

Demarest, David P. Jr., gen. ed. *"The River Ran Red": Homestead 1892* (Pittsburgh: University of Pittsburgh Press, 1992).

DeMaria, Alfred. *How Management Wins Union Organizing Campaigns* (New York: Executive Enterprises Publications, 1980).

Detroit Sunday Journal, Mar. 9, 1997, 10.

Dorsey, George. "The Bayonne Refinery Strike of 1915–1916." *Polish American Studies* 33 (1976).

Drew, Frank. "The Present Farmers' Movement." *Political Science Quarterly* 6 (June 1891).

Drummond, Bob. "Clinton Strike Policy Upheld." *Chicago Sun-Times*, Aug. 1, 1995, 46.

D. S. "Industrial Spying in Trade Unions." *Workers Age*, Jan. 1938, 8.

Dubofsky, Melvyn. *We Shall Be All: A History of the Industrial Workers of the World* (New York: Quadrangle Books/New York Times Book Company, 1969).

―――. "Abortive Reform: The Wilson Administration and Organized Labor, 1913–1920." In *Work, Community, and Power,* ed. James E. Cronin and Carmen Siriann (Philadelphia: Temple University Press, 1983).

Duchez, Louis. "Victory at McKees Rocks." *International Socialist Review,* Oct. 1909, 290.

Dulles, Foster Rhea, and Melvyn Dubofsky. *Labor in America: A History* (Arlington Heights, Ill.: Harlan Davidson, 1984).

Eastmen, Max. "Class War in Colorado." *The Masses,* June 1914, 7.

Eisler, Kim Isaac. "Secret Service Inc." *Washingtonian* 31 (May 1996): 48–49.

Electric Railway Review, May 18, 1907, 658.

"Employers' Turn on the Stand." *Business Week,* Nov. 9, 1957, 32.

"The End of a Futile Strike." *Outlook,* Apr. 30, 1910, 963.

"Farley Breaks up Strikebreakers Camp." *American Federationist* 15 (Feb. 1908): 116–17.

Fink, Gary M. "Labor Espionage: The Fulton Bag and Cotton Mills Strike of 1914–1915." *Labor's Heritage* 1 (Apr. 1989).

―――. *The Fulton Bag and Cotton Mills Strike of 1914–15: Espionage, Labor Conflict, and New South Industrial Relations* (Ithaca, N.Y.: ILR Press, 1993).

Fink, Walter. *The Ludlow Massacre* (Denver: Williamson-Haffner Publishers, 1915; rpt., Leon Stein and Philip Taft, eds., *Massacre at Ludlow: Four Reports* [New York: Arno and New York Times, 1971]).

"Fink Racket: Report on Strike-breaking Prepared by the La Follette Civil Liberties Committee." *Nation,* Feb. 11, 1939, 165.

"Firms Learn Art of Keeping Unions Out." *Wall Street Journal,* Apr. 19, 1977, 48.

Fitch, John. "When a Sheriff Breaks a Strike." *Survey* 34 (July 1915): 414.

Foner, Philip S. *History of the Labor Movement in the United States: The Policies and Practices of the American Federation of Labor, 1900–1909* (New York: International Publishers, 1964).

―――. *Labor Songs of the Nineteenth Century* (Urbana: University of Illinois Press, 1975).

―――. *History of the Labor Movement in the United States: The Industrial Workers of the World, 1905–1917,* vol. 4 (New York: International Publishers, 1980).

―――. *History of the Labor Movement in the United States: On the Eve of America's Entrance into World War I, 1915–1916* (New York: International Publishers, 1982).

Fones-Wolf, Elizabeth A. *Selling Free Enterprise: The Business Assault on Labor and Liberalism. 1945–1960* (Urbana: University of Illinois Press, 1994).

"For Labor, For Management, For Shefferman." *Newsweek,* Nov. 4, 1957, 33.

Fredricks, B. T. "James Farley, Strike-breaker." *Leslie's Magazine* 59 (May 1905).

Freeman, Richard. "Why Unions are Faring Poorly in N.L.R.B. Elections." In

Thomas A. Cochran, ed., *Challenges and Choices Facing American Labor* (Cambridge: MIT Press, 1985).

Friedman, Morris. *The Pinkerton Labor Spy* (New York: Wilshire Book Co., 1907).

Fulmer, William E. "When Employees Want to Oust their Union." *Harvard Business Review* 56 (Mar.–Apr. 1978).

Gall, Gilbert J. "Heber Blankenhorn, the La Follette Committee and the Irony of Industrial Repression." *Labor History* 23 (spring 1982).

Gavett, Thomas W. *Development of the Labor Movement in Milwaukee* (Madison: University of Wisconsin Press, 1965).

"The General Strike in Philadelphia." *Current Literature* 48 (Apr. 1910): 363.

"Gompers Speaks for Labor." *McClure's Magazine*, Feb. 1912, 372.

Graige, John H. "The Professional Strikebreaker." *Collier's Weekly*, Dec. 3, 1910, 20.

———. "The Violent Art of Strikebreaking." *Collier's Weekly*, Jan. 7, 1911, 29.

Green, James R. *The World of the Worker: Labor in Twentieth-Century America* (New York: Hill and Wang, 1980).

———. "Tying the Knot of Solidarity: The Pittston Strike of 1989–1990." In John M. Laslett, ed., *The United Mine Workers of America: A Model of Industrial Solidarity* (University Park: Pennsylvania State University Press, 1996), 519.

Gribble, Richard. *Catholicism and the San Francisco Labor Movement, 1896–1921* (San Francisco: Mellen Research University Press, 1993).

Griffin, Robert P. Address to the Labor Law Section of the Michigan State Bar, Annual Meeting, Sept. 25, 1959.

Grow, Doug. "Behemoth Pepsi Short on Gratitude." *Star Tribune*, Aug. 20, 2000, 2B.

Gutman, Herbert G. "The Braidwood Lockout of 1874." *Journal of the Illinois State Historical Society* 53 (1960): 18–19.

Hadsell, Richard M., and William E. Coffee. "From Law and Order to Class Warfare: Baldwin-Felts Detectives in the Southern West Virginia Coal Fields." *West Virginia History* 40 (spring 1979).

Hammond, John Hays. *Hammond: The Autobiography of John Hays Hammond*, vol. 1 (New York: Farrar and Rinehart Incorporated, 1935).

Harris, Evelyn, and Frank Krebs. *From Humble Beginnings: West Virginia State Federation of Labor, 1903–1957* (Charleston: West Virginia Labor History Publishing Fund, 1960).

Headlee, Thomas J. Jr. "The Richmond Streetcar Strike of 1903." *Virginia Cavalcade* 25, no. 4 (spring 1976).

Heaster, Randolph. "Strikers Walk; Security Watches." *Kansas City Star*, June 6, 1997. B1.

Hennen, R. V., and D. D. Teets Jr., *Fayette County* (Wheeling: Wheeling News Litho Company, 1919).

Hinds, Michael deCourcy. "Bitter Coal Strike May Be at End." *New York Times*, Dec. 23, 1989, 17.

Hoerr, John. "A Host of Strikebreakers is Tipping the Scales Against Labor." *Business Week*, July 15, 1985, 32.

Hogg, J. Barnard. "Public Reaction to Pinkertonism and the Labor Question." *Pennsylvania History* 11 (1944).

Hopkins, Gordon. "The Labor Spy." *Social Action*, June 15, 1937, 11.

Horan, James D. *The Pinkertons: The Detective Dynasty that Made History* (New York: Crown Publishers, 1967).

Howard, Sidney. *The Labor Spy* (New York: Republic Publishing Company, 1924).

Huberman, Leo. *The Labor Spy Racket* (New York: Modern Age Books, 1937).

Hunter, Robert. *Violence and the Labor Movement* (New York: Macmillan Company, 1914).

Hutchinson, John. *The Imperfect Union: A History of Corruption in American Trade Unions* (New York: E. P. Dutton and Company, 1972).

Hyde, Charles K. "Undercover and Underground: Labor Spies and Mine Management in the Early Twentieth Century." *Business History Review* 60 (spring 1986): 1–27.

"Industrial Policing and Espionage." *Harvard Law Review* 52 (Mar. 1939).

Industrial Union Bulletin, Mar. 9, 1907.

Ingham, John. "A Strike in the Progressive Era: McKees Rocks, 1909." *Pennsylvania Magazine of History and Biography* 90, no. 3 (July 1966).

The Interchurch World Movement. *The Commission of Inquiry, Report on Steel Strike of 1919* (New York: Harcourt, Brace and Company, 1920).

———. *Public Opinion and the Steel Strike: Supplementary Reports of the Investigators to the Commission of Inquiry* (New York: Harcourt, Brace and Company, 1921).

Jeffreys-Jones, Rhodri. "Profit Over Class: A Study in American Espionage." *Journal of American Studies* 6 (1972): 238–48.

———. "Violence in American History: Plug Uglies in the Progressive Era." In Bernard Bailyn and Donald Flemming, eds., *Perspective in American History*, vol. 8 (Cambridge: Harvard University Press, Charles Warren Center for Studies in American History, 1974).

———. *Violence and Reform in American History* (New York: New Viewpoints, 1978).

Jensen, Vernon H. *Heritage of Conflict: Labor Relations in the Nonferrous Metals Industry up to 1930* (Ithaca: Cornell University Press, 1950).

Johnson, Judy. "Cleveland Teachers Beat Union Busters." *People's Weekly World*, Sept. 21, 1996, 1.

Johnson, Tom. "Caterpillar Bulldozes the United Auto Workers." *Business and Society Review* 96 (1996): 39.

Kahn, Albert E. *High Treason: The Plot Against the People* (New York: Lear Publishers, 1950).

Kasindorf, Martin. "Exec. Order Bars Hiring Replacements." *Newsday*, Mar. 9, 1995, A17.

Kazin, Michael. *Barons of Labor: The San Francisco Building Trades and Union Power in the Progressive Era* (Urbana: University of Illinois Press, 1987).

Kellogg, Paul U. "The McKees Rocks Strike." *Survey*, Aug. 7, 1909, 656–57.

Kelly, Kevin. "Picket Lines? Just Call 1–800 Strikebreaker." *Business Week*, Mar. 27, 1995, 42.

Kilborn, Peter T. "California Strike Becomes a Battle over Permanent Job Replacements." *New York Times*, Apr. 17, 1994.

Kimball, Gregg D. "The Working People of Richmond: Life and Labor in an Industrial City, 1865–1920." *Labor's Heritage* 3, no. 2 (Apr. 1991).

Knight, Robert E. L. *Industrial Relations in the San Francisco Bay Area, 1900–1918* (Berkeley: University of California Press, 1960).

"Labor Fights Back Against Union Busters." *U.S. News and World Report*, Dec. 10, 1979, 98.

Labor in America. *"We Won't Go Back": UMWA/Pittston Strike, 1989–90* (Clinchco, Va.: Dickenson Star, 1990).

Lagerfield, Steve. "To Break a Union." *Harper's*, May 1981, 16.

Lane, Winthrop D. *Civil War in West Virginia: A Story of Industrial Conflict in the Coal Mines* (New York: B. W. Huebsch, 1921).

———. "Labor Spy in West Virginia." *Survey*, October 22, 1921, 111.

Lee, Howard B. *Bloodletting in Appalachia: The Story of West Virginia's Four Major Mine Wars and Other Thrilling Incidents of Its Coal Fields* (Morgantown: West Virginia University Press, 1969).

Leonard, Stephen J. "Bloody August: The Denver Tramway Strike of 1920." *Colorado Heritage* (summer 1985): 18–31.

Levinson, Edward. *I Break Strikes! The Technique of Pearl L. Bergoff* (New York: Robert M. McBride and Company, 1935; rpt., New York: Arno and New York Times, 1969).

———. "The Right to Break Strikes." *Current History* 45 (Feb. 1937): 81.

———. "Strikebreaking Incorporated." *Harper's Magazine*, Nov. 1937, 724.

Levitt, Martin J., with Terry Conrow. *Confessions of a Union Buster* (New York: Crown Publishers, 1983).

Lewis, Diana E. "Temporary Nursing Agency Gives Massachusetts Hospitals Options amid Strikes." *Boston Globe*, Apr. 6, 2000.

Lingenfelter, Richard E. *The Hardrock Miners: A History of the Labor Mining*

Movement in the American West, 1863–1893 (Berkeley: University of California Press, 1974).

Lublin, Joanne. "Labor Strikes Back at Consultants that Help Firms Keep Unions Out." *Wall Street Journal,* Apr. 2, 1981.

Lunt, Richard D. *Law and Order vs. the Miners: West Virginia, 1907–1933* (Hamden, Conn.: Archon, 1979).

Lynch, Lawrence. "The West Virginia Coal Strike." *Political Science Quarterly* 39 (Dec. 1914).

Mangold, W. P. "On the Labor Front." *New Republic,* Oct. 3, 1934, 213.

McCartin, Joseph A. *Labor's Great War* (Chapel Hill: University of North Carolina Press, 1997).

McClellan, John L. *Crime Without Punishment* (New York: Duell, Sloan and Pearce, 1962).

McCloin, John Bernard. *San Francisco: The Story of a City* (San Rafael, Calif.: Presidio Press, 1978).

McCormick, Kyle. *The New-Kanawha River and the Mine War of West Virginia* (Charleston: Mathews Printing and Lithography Company, 1959).

McDonald, Dwight. "Espionage Inc." *Nation,* Feb. 27, 1937, 239.

"McDonnell Workers File Charges with NLRB." UPI, July 3, 1996, BC cycle.

McGovern, George S., and Leonard F. Guttridge. *The Great Coalfield War* (Boston: Houghton, Mifflin Company, 1972).

McMurry, Donald L. *The Great Burlington Strike of 1888: A Case History in Labor Relations* (Cambridge, Mass.: Harvard University Press, 1956).

McNames, J. F. "Spies and Traitors." *Brotherhood of Locomotive Firemen and Engineer's Magazine,* Feb. 1909, 446–52.

McQuiston, F. B. "The Strike-breakers." *Independent* 17 (Oct. 17, 1901): 2456.

Maney, Patrick J. *"Young Bob" La Follette: A Biography of Robert M. La Follette Jr., 1895–1953* (Columbia: University of Missouri Press, 1978).

Meloney, William Brown. "Strikebreaking as a Profession." *Public Opinion* 38 (Mar. 1905): 441.

Mishra, Raja. "To Serve and Protect—For a Price." *Detroit Journal,* Aug. 4, 1995.

Molloy, Scott. *Trolley Wars: Streetcar Workers on the Line* (Washington, D.C.: Smithsonian Institution Press, 1996).

Mooney, Fred. *Struggle in the Coal Fields: The Autobiography of Fred Mooney.* Ed. J. W. Hess (Morgantown: West Virginia University Library, 1967).

Moore, Marat. "Women's Stories from the Pittston Strike." *Now and Then: The Appalachian Magazine,* (fall 1990): 33.

Morn, Frank. *The Eye that Never Sleeps: A History of the Pinkerton National Detective Agency* (Bloomington: Indiana University Press, 1982).

"Now Employers Are Under Fire." *U.S. News and World Report,* Nov. 1, 1957, 95.

Ozanne, Robert. *A Century of Labor-Management Relations at McCormick and International Harvester* (Madison: University of Wisconsin Press, 1967).

Papanikolas, Zeese. *Buried Unsung: Louis Tikas and the Ludlow Massacre* (Salt Lake City: University of Utah Press, 1982).

Pate, James L. "Guerrilla War in the Hills: Mercs Come to Appalachia." *Soldier of Fortune,* Sept. 1986.

"Petition to the President for a Federal Commission." *Survey,* Dec. 30, 1911, 1431.

"Philadelphia Strike and Settlement." *Motorman and Conductor* 17 (June 1909), 4–6.

Pinkerton, Allan. *Tests on Passenger Conductors Made by the National Police Agency* (Chicago: George H. Fergus, 1867).

———. *Strikers, Communists, Tramps, and Detectives* (New York: G. W. Carleton and Company, 1878).

———. *Professional Thieves and the Detective* (New York: G. W. Carleton and Company, 1880).

"Pinkerton's Men." *Nation,* Jan. 27, 1887, 70.

Rickard, T. A. *A History of American Mining* (New York: McGraw-Hill, 1932).

Savage, Lon. *Thunder in the Mountains: The West Virginia Mine Wars, 1920–1921* (Pittsburgh: University of Pittsburgh Press, 1990).

Sawey, Orlan. *Siringo* (Boston: Twayne Publishers, 1981).

Scott, Leroy. "'Strikebreaking' as a New Occupation." *World's Work 10;* (May 1905): 6200.

"Senate Probings." *Personnel Journal,* Mar. 1938, 288.

Sesek, Grant. "Asarco: Strike Guards Working without Licenses." *Helena (Montana) Independent Record,* Feb. 24, 1999.

Shalloo, Jeremiah Patrick. *Private Police: With a Special Reference to Pennsylvania* (Philadelphia: American Academy of Political and Social Science, 1933).

Shefferman, Nathan W., with Dale Kramer. *The Man in the Middle* (Garden City, N.Y.: Doubleday and Company, 1961).

Sherefkin, Robert. "JCI Beefs Up Security at Taylor Plant." *Crain's Detroit Business,* Feb. 10, 1997.

"Sheriff Kinkead's Busy Day." *Literary Digest,* Aug. 1915, 256–61.

Shorrock, Tim. "Steel Workers Reach Pact." *Journal of Commerce,* Nov. 6, 1996, 5A.

Silver, Christopher. *Twentieth Century Richmond: Planning, Politics, and Race* (Knoxville: University of Tennessee Press, 1984).

Sinclair, Gladys M. *Bayonne Old and New: The City of Diversified Industry* (New York: Marantha Publishers, 1940).

Siringo, Charles A. *A Cowboy Detective: A True Story of Twenty-Two Years With a World-Famous Detective Agency* (Chicago: W. B. Conkey, 1912; rpt., Lincoln: University of Nebraska Press, 1988).

———. *Rita and Spurs: The Story of a Lifetime Spent in the Saddle as a Cowboy Detective* (New York: Houghton Mifflin Company, 1927).

———. *Two Evilisms: Pinkertonism and Anarchism* (Austin, Tex.: Steck-Vaughn Company, 1968).

Smith, Rufus. "Some Phases of the McKees Rocks Strike." *Survey,* Oct. 2, 1909.

Spaeth, Sigmund. *Weep Some More My Lady* (Garden City, N.Y.: n.p., 1927).

Spielman, J. E. *The Stool Pigeon and the Open Shop Movement* (Minneapolis: American Publishing Co., 1923), 142–43.

Sprague, Stuart S. "Unionization Struggles on Paint Creek and Cabin Creek, 1912–1913." *West Virginia History* 38 (1977).

"Spy Profits." *Literary Digest,* Mar. 27, 1937, 5.

St. Paul, Virginia. "Christians and the Coalfield Conflict." *Christian Century,* Oct. 4, 1989, 869.

Stone, Melville E. *Fifty Years a Journalist* (New York: Doubleday, 1921).

"Strikebreaking." *Fortune,* Jan. 1935, 58.

"Struggle over Striker Replacements." *Baltimore Sun,* Mar. 16, 1995, 16A.

Swoboda, Frank. "On a Mission to Find Security in the Protection Business." *Washington Post,* May 26, 1996, F11.

Swoboda, Frank, and Helen Dewar. "Labor Makes Startling Offer to Congress." *Los Angeles Times,* June 11, 1992, D4.

Time, June 10, 1940, 19.

"To Make Employers Fight Fair: Oppressive Labor Practices Act of 1939." *New Republic,* May 3, 1939, 365.

Torry, Jack. "Reich Wants to Ban Hiring Striker Replacements." *Pittsburg Post-Gazette,* Mar. 31, 1993, B12.

Vance, Charles F. "Picture-Perfect Strike Protection." *Security Management* 35, no. 11 (Nov. 1991): 47.

Wade, Louise Carroll. *Chicago's Pride: The Stockyards, Packingtown, and Environs in the Nineteenth Century* (Urbana: University of Illinois Press, 1987).

Warrum, Henry. *Peace Officers and Detectives: The Law of Sheriffs, Constables, Marshalls, Municipal Police, and Detectives* (Greenfield, Ind.: William Mitchell, 1895).

Weinstein, James. *The Corporate Ideal in the Liberal State, 1900–1918* (Boston: Beacon Press, 1969).

Weiss, Robert P. "Private Detective Agencies and Labour Discipline in the United States 1855–1946." *Historical Journal* 29 (Mar. 1986).

Werstein, Irving. *Strangled Voices: The Story of the Haymarket Affair* (New York: McMillian Company, 1969).

West, Harold E. "Civil War in the West Virginia Coal Mines." *Survey,* Apr. 5, 1913, 43–45.

"What Senators Hear About Union-Busting." *U.S. News and World Report,* Nov. 1957, 110.

"Wilkes-Barre Strike Settled." *Electric Railway Journal* 48, Dec. 23, 1916, 1312–13.

Willits, Joseph. "The Conclusions and Recommendations of the U.S. Coal Commission as to Labor Relations in Bituminous Coal Mining." *Annals of the American Academy of Political Science* 3 (1924): 97–109.

Witte, Edwin E. *The Government in Labor Disputes* (New York: McGraw-Hill Book Company, 1932; rpt., New York: Arno and New York Times, 1969).

Wolf, Leon. *Lockout: The Story of the Homestead Strike of 1892: A Study of Violence, Unionism, and the Carnegie Steel Empire* (New York: Harper and Row, 1965).

Workers Defense League. *Labor Defense and Democracy* (New York: n.p., 1941).

Yancy, Dwayne. "Thunder in The Coal Fields: The UMW's Strike Against Pittston." *Roanoke Times and World News,* Apr. 29, 1990, 8.

Young, Art. *Art Young: His Life and Times* (New York: Sheridan House, 1939).

Zieger, Robert. *American Workers, American Unions, 1920–1985* (Baltimore: Johns Hopkins University Press, 1986).

INDEX

Note: page numbers in italics refer to illustrations

CPSIA information can be obtained
at www.ICGtesting.com
Printed in the USA
LVHW090154201121
703869LV00010B/75

9 780821 414668